ART AND HISTORY
MILAN

BONECHI

Publication created and designed by *Casa Editrice Bonechi*
Picture research: *Francesco Giannoni*
Graphic design and layout: *Serena de Leonardis*
Make up: *Rita Bianucci*
Cover: *Sonia Gottardo*
Text: *Patrizia Fabbri, Rina Bucci*
Translation: *Paula Boomsliter*
Editing: *Patrizia Fabbri*
Illustrations: *Stefano Benini*
Map: *Centro Studi Tecnici, Sesto Fiorentino, Firenze*

© Copyright by Casa Editrice Bonechi,via Cairoli 18/b, Firenze - Italia
Tel +39 055 576841 - Fax +39 055 5000766

E-mail: bonechi@bonechi.it – Internet: www.bonechi.com

Printed in Italy by *Centro Stampa Editoriale Bonechi.*

The majority of the photographs are property of the *Casa Editrice Bonechi* Archives.
They were taken by
Gaetano Barone, Serena de Leonardis, Di Giovine Fotografica, Foto Saporetti, Mario Ingrosso, Dante Pini, Veneranda Fabbrica Duomo di Milano.

Other photographs were provided by
Atlantide (authorization S.M.A. n. 01-295 - 21/06/95): pages 54, 70 below, 110 above left.
Atlantide/Stefano Amantini: pages 30 the second from the top, and below right and left, 117 above right.
Atlantide/Guido Cozzi: pages 9 below right, 16 above right, 18 below, 24 below, 27 below, 30 above, 42 above, 114.
© *Foto Scala Firenze*: pages 33 above left and below, 78-79, 99 below.
Mario Ingrosso: pages 28 above and below left, 69 below, 95, 96 above.
Photoland-Travelpress: page 98 above.
Antonio Quattrone: pages 57-64.
Ghigo Roli: pages 8 below left, above left and above right, 9 above left, above right, the second from the top, 10-11, 13 above, 17, 18 above, 20, 22, 23 below, 24 above left, 30 the third from the top, 34 below right, 38, 39 below, 42 center and below, 43 left, 44-45, 49, 50 center and below left, 52, 65 above left, 66, 67 above, 68 above and below right, 71, 75 above, 76, 81 above, 82, 97 above, 99 above, 101 below, 102 center, 103 below right, 105 below right, 107 above, 109, 110 below, 111 center, 113, 116 below, 123 above right, 125 above.

The publisher apologises for any omissions and is willing to make amends with the formal recognition of the author of any photo subsequently identified.

ISBN 88-476-1438-4

• • •

Introduction

Founded by the Insubres Gauls probably in the early 4th century BC, the ancient *Mediolanum* (a name that according to some sources means "city between two rivers" and according to others "city at the center of the plain") was in the beginning just a small settlement. It grew rapidly following its conquest by Rome in 222 BC, clinched in 197 BC after a period of rebellion at the time of the invasion of Italy by Hannibal and the Carthaginian armies. As the capital of the 11th Augustan region (Transpadana), an important and strategic trade node enclosed by a first circle of walls, the city attained its maximum splendor in 292 AD, when Emperor Maximianus chose it as capital of the Western Roman Empire, strengthened its fortifications, and moved his court there. It was there that in 313 Emperor Constantine issued his famous Edict; there that Bishop Ambrose worked to firmly oppose Arianism after coming to Milan in 370 as a layman in the guise of imperial gover-

nor. The decay of the Empire and the menace posed by the barbarian hordes (Alaric's Visigoths in 401, Teodoric's Ostrogoths in 489, and so on through the Goths, who despite strenuous resistance by the Byzantines sacked and devastated the city in 539) marked the rapid decline of prosperous Milan, which in 569 was occupied by Alboin's Longobards and lost its supremacy in the region in favor of nearby Pavia. Such a position of inferiority and increasingly marked political isolation persisted under the Franks and the Carolingians, but two great forces contributed, in that era, to shoring up Milan's opportunities and fortune: flourishing trade and the figure of the archbishop, an office which over time had succeeded in reinforcing and strengthening its prestige and power in the political sphere. One bishop in particular, Ariberto di Intimiano (11th century), maneuvering among feudal lords and commoners, even succeeded in defying the emperor and thus

An ancient map of Milan from the Bertarelli Collection.

in a certain sense laying the groundwork for a slow reawakening of Milan and its return to prominence. The short-term upshot of such tactics was to assure that although the archbishop remained the supreme authority in the city, Milan was constituted as a commune or free city in 1117, with the wealthy bourgeoisie officially called to participate in local government. Shortly, the city's economic power increased dramatically, to the point of permitting it to absorb the surrounding territory and substantially replace the pre-existing feudal organization; its expansionist horizons also broadened, to the detriment of nearby centers like Como and Lodi. The intention was to create a truly independent state, and to this end Milan took advantage of the momentary disinterest manifested by the imperial dynasty, involved as it was, in Germany, in fierce struggles for succession. But when Frederick Bar-

barossa, returned to power, decided to reinforce his theretofore weakened hegemony over the Italian peninsula, he was able to exploit the general malcontent and the consequent support of the communes under Milan's rule. He put the city under siege and finally, in 1162, took it and razed it to the ground. Milan rose again rapidly, however, and in time to turn the nearby cities' discontent with imperial rule to its own advantage. And thus these cities joined Milan in the Lombard League founded on the Oath of Pontida; the League emerged from the 1176 Battle of Legnano with a legendary victory over the imperial troops. Communal independence was thus permanently reaffirmed, but the continuing internal conflicts that irremediably marked the political proximity of the various Communes assured the region only a lengthy—and dangerous—period of instability. This situation persisted until once again an archbishop—this time Ottone Visconti, who in 1277—after prolonged and bloody conflicts with other important Milanese families—succeeded in imposing his hegemony over the city, throwing open the doors to power in Milan to his nephew Matteo and Matteo's grandson Azzone. Thus began that protracted (130 years) period of Visconti rule that on the one hand marked the beginning of the real—and quite determined—rebirth of the city, which went on to return to great pomp and splendor, but on the other was characterized by violent dynastic struggles. All things considered, we may say that the Visconti family considered Milan and its holdings (which progressively expanded toward Piemonte, Emilia and Liguria) as personal property, to be handed down and subdivided generation after generation. This explains, for example, why in the mid-14th century the territory was managed by the two brothers Galeazzo II and Bernabò. But in 1378, when Galeazzo II was succeeded by his son Gian Galeazzo, this union became extremely unwieldy—to the point that the man who was destined to become one of Milan's most important and brilliant lords did not hesitate an instant to brutally eliminate his uncle and his uncle's heirs. At the death of Gian Galeazzo, who acquired the title of duke in 1395, the situation came to a head due to the rivalry among Gian Galeazzo's three heirs and the increasing power of a number of ambitious mercenaries. One of these, a certain Francesco Sforza, husband of the last of the Visconti's, Bianca Maria, after the brief interlude of the Ambrosian Republic ushered in a new period of peace and prosperity, becoming lord of the city by public acclaim in 1450. Francesco, who turned out to be a far-sighted prince and a capable administrator, did all he could to ensure peace among the various Italian states and the well-being of the city he governed. The same cannot be said for his successors, including that Ludovico I il Moro ("the Moor") who, exploiting the premature death by violence of his

The portraits of Francesco Sforza and his wife Bianca Maria Visconti, attributed to Bonifacio Bembo.

brother, Galeazzo Maria, and the hesitation of the widow, Bona of Savoia, succeeded first in obtaining tutelage of his very young nephew, Gian Galeazzo Maria, and then, at his death, absolute power. Ludovico was a munificent lord; during his reign, Milan's city fabric developed considerably and the economy thrived. But his foreign policy, which reflected his ambitious expansionistic aims, only procured continual wars and an uninterrupted intrigue of alliances and rivalries that in time proved to constitute an element of intrinsic weakness that in the end had serious repercussions on the future of the city. To suffer the consequences were above all the descendents of Ludovico, who watched as the duchy weakened and then rapidly fell to pieces as it was contested by the French and the Spanish, who, in 1535, at the death of Francesco II, the last of the Sforza family, took power over Milan and its territories. Spanish domination, exercised by a governor, was for the city a long period of impoverishment and economic and political stagnancy marked by abuse of power by the local aristocracy, heavy taxes, and even two terrible plagues in 1576 and 1629-1633. And once again it was the archbishopric (this time, guided by the extraordinary Saint Charles and Federico Borromeo) and the city's incredible economic power and vitality that saved it from catastrophe. When the Austrians replaced the Spaniards in 1737, the situation reached a turning point. From the very first, the new government implemented a policy of centralization in the best absolutist tradition, a policy that designated Venice as the center of power and relegated Milan to the uncomfortable role of passive satellite. But Austrian dominion also brought to the city (and to Lombardy in general) reforms aimed at improving the standard of living of the people and the economy of the territories. What is more, in the wake of Viennese prestige Milan slowly reacquired a meaningful role in Europe, at least on the cultural plane. Great thinkers and the Illuminist philosophers found Milan to be a particularly favorable habitat; literary societies flourished and with time took on a political valence. Think, for example, of poets like Parini, or of the works of Cesare Beccaria, who with his *On Crimes and Punishments* laid a milestone for European civilization—and so on down through the imposing figure of Alessandro Manzoni. As time passed, the Lombard peoples began to feel the weight of Austrian supremacy as a despotically-imposed and oppressive yoke. This feeling was perhaps incensed by the revolutionary parenthesis initiated by the French governors, who between 1796 and 1815 saw the institution of the Cisalpine Republic first and then the Kingdom of Italy,

following on the new egalitarian and liberal ideas. A victorious Napoleon had entered Milan on 15 May 1796, and in Milan, on 26 May 1805, was crowned ruler of the new kingdom, whose government he had entrusted to his stepson and viceroy Eugène de Beauharnais. But Austrian dominion was restored in 1815, at the fall of Napoleon; and although it was more onerous and less well-tolerated than ever, entered into crisis only in 1848, with the revolts and the mythical Five Days of Milan, when the city's populace rose and opted for annexation to the Kingdom of Sardinia.

This glorious attempt, however, foundered when Carlo Alberto di Savoia was defeated by the Hapsburg armies. Milan thus had to await 8 June 1859 and the triumphal entry into the city of Vittorio Emanuele II and Napoleon III (a historical event prepared with consummate political skill by Cavour) to officially declare the end of Austrian dominion over Lombardy and the region's entry, in perfect order, into the new unified Italy. Shortly thereafter, Milan became the new Italy's economic capital—and, in a certain sense, its cultural capital as well. The city saw rapid and peremptory urban development, a significant increase in population, and alacritous industrial growth; it consequently took on a role at the social avant-garde that was to make it the nerve center of the first Socialist revendications. Following WW1 and the Fascist period, during which time the city proved from the very beginning to be a center of the active and well-organized underground movement, thanks in part to the support of conspicuous political and cultural figures, WW2 inflicted deep and devastating wounds on the city. The repeated aerial bombings—and in particular the tremendous incursions of August 1943—totally destroyed vast areas of the city. After the armistice, during the period of German occupation and until the city was liberated on 25 April 1945, Milan was one of the most important and active centers of the Partisan movement. Following the war, the always-vital and enterprising Milan imperatively reawakened and reaffirmed its role as economic capital of Italy and as a guiding force in a myriad of sectors: industry, city planning, culture, and the social sphere.

The Corsia dei Servi (today's Corso Vittorio Emanuele), enlarged in the early 19th century, in a painting by Giuseppe Canella.

The French entering Milan, in an engraving by C. Vernet.

Piazza del Duomo

Almost as though it were the hub, or the central core, from which the entire fabric of the city irradiates, the broad, elegant rectangle in the center of Milan that is the splendid Piazza del Duomo, drawn at the foot of the cathedral, opens out to lend perspective to this great monument and accentuate its majesty. When in 1859 construction of the cathedral seemed to have been (finally) almost concluded, the City of Milan called a public competition for building the square in front of it. There were 176 bidders. The winner was Giuseppe Mengoni, whose plan changed the face of the area and was so all-embracing as to absorb almost 40% of the entire city budget for about 20 years. The resulting square is framed by buildings specifically designed to offset the cathedral: on the north side we have the *Palazzo Settentrionale*, and on the south the *Palazzo Meridionale*. Both have porticoes. The first is broken by the arch of triumph that is the monumental access to the *Galleria Vittorio Emanuele II*; the second is flanked by the so-called "propylaea": two smaller buildings, with loggias, begun in 1939, damaged in the 1943 bombings, and completed in 1956. On the west side, instead, there rises the *Palazzo dell'Orologio*. At the center of the square we have the *equestrian statue of Vittorio Emanuele II* created by Ercole Rosa and inaugurated in 1896; the statue represents the king in the act of reining in his horse to turn to urge on his troops at the battle of San Martino. Authentic treasures lie even below the square: in 1942, excavations brought to light remains of the *Basilica of Santa Tecla*, and we know that the remains of the ancient *Cathedral of Santa Maria Maggiore* are still hidden under the massive Duomo.

Two views, one by day and the other by night, of Piazza del Duomo, the vital "central core" of the capital of the Lombardy region. The square was designed to exalt the majesty of the cathedral.

The Duomo

The majestic cathedral of Milan, dedicated to "Maria Nascente" and today one of the world's largest churches, was begun in the second half of the 14th century—but the work went on for five centuries.

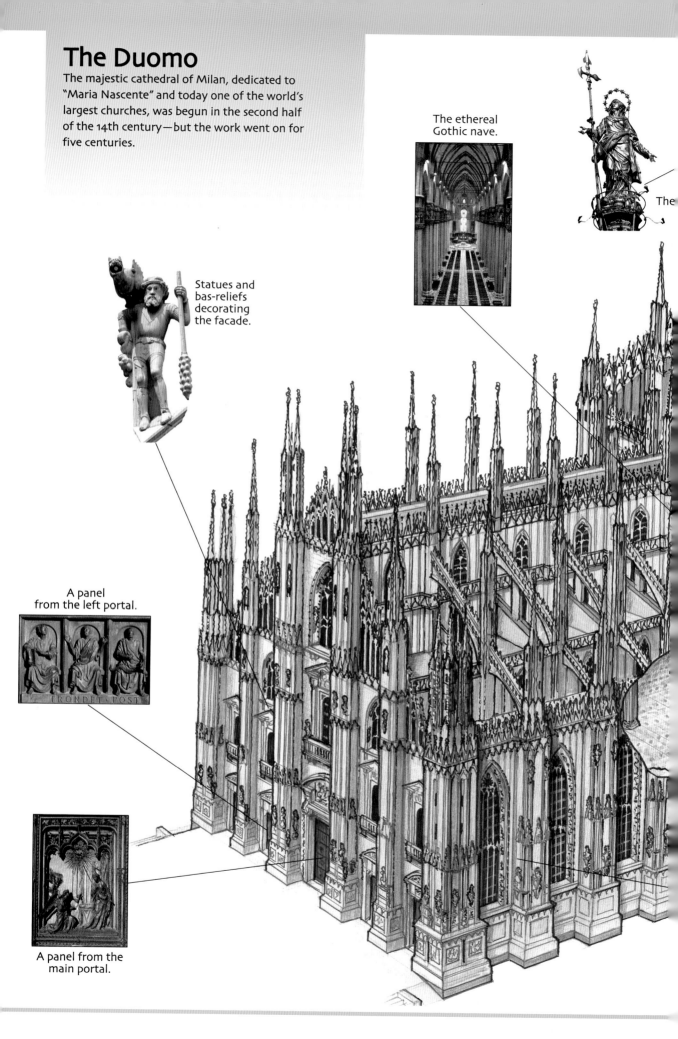

The ethereal Gothic nave.

The

Statues and bas-reliefs decorating the facade.

A panel from the left portal.

A panel from the main portal.

The apse seen from one of the terraces of the Duomo.

The rose-window of the apse with the *razza*, symbol of Gian Galeazzo Visconti.

The portal of the south sacristy.

Ariberto of Intimiano's crucifix (the original is in the Museo del Duomo).

The crypt.

The multicolor windows of the apse.

The Duomo

The true heart and religious symbol of the city, the world's third-largest church in terms of covered area—157 meters in length and 92 in width at the transept—after only Saint Peter's in the Vatican and the Seville cathedral, Milan's Duomo is Italy's most perfect example of flamboyant Gothic. Its construction was a long and extremely complex process. The area selected for the cathedral had, since the 4th century, hosted religious buildings of various sorts: the *Basilica of Santa Tecla*, the summer cathedral demolished in the 15th century; the characteristic octagonal *Baptistery of San Giovanni delle Fonti*; and above all the ancient Romanesque *Cathedral of Santa Maria Maggiore* (9th century), the winter cathedral, first incorporated and then finally—and magnificently—replaced by today's Duomo dedicated to "Maria Nascente." The original plan was drawn up, probably by an unknown transalpine architect of the purest Gothic school, on commission by the then-archbishop Antonio da Saluzzo. The archbishop was supported in his ambitious plan by Gian Galeazzo Visconti—who granted tax exemptions and free-of-cost exploitation of the Candoglia marble quarries—and by the pope himself, Boniface IX. In 1386, the great Duomo worksite began to bustle with workers, who in just a couple of years, under the supervision of Simone di Orsenigo and

The Duomo, with two of the many statues that adorn the facade.

the masters Marco da Campione and Giovannino de' Grassi, both from Como, had completed the lower plinth. Work then centered on the area of the apse, the first part of the actual cathedral to be raised, and moved slowly toward the facade. Until the beginning of the 1400's the worksite was contained under the roof of the pre-existing cathedral, and supervision of construction fell to a series of more or less famous figures: the Frenchman Nicolas de Bonaventure, Johann of Freiburg, Giovanni of Campione, Johann of Fernach, Heinrich of Gmünden, Ulrich of Fussingen, Bernardo of Venezia, Gabriele Stornaloco, Giovannino de' Grassi, Jean Mignot, Filippino degli Organi, Giovanni and Guiniforte Solari, Filarete, and Johannes Nexenperger. And as the influence of so many masters slowly altered the original plan, the building became progressively more spectacular and majestic. The enormous costs of the work were met by the donations of noble families (not only Milanese) and public subscriptions, but the decisive impetus was given by the contributions first of the Visconti and later the Sforza family. In 1418, when construction of the nave and aisles had just begun, Pope Martin V consecrated the high altar and the church. The towering tambour dates to the last thirty years of the 15th century: it was begun by Solari and completed by Giovanni Antonio Amadeo, and benefited from the contributions of great "experts" like Leonardo da Vinci and Luca Fancelli. After a period of stasis, work resumed with new vigor in 1527 under Saint Charles Borromeo, but two centuries were to elapse before the roof was completely covered with stone slabs to form that sort of spectacular terrace on which, today, we can walk to admire marvelous views of the city. It was only in 1885 that the remarkable forest of dizzying spires, the first of which dates to 1404, could have been said to have been completed. The final result was an extraordinary building punctuated by 40 buttresses pierced by tall windows, with a short transept and an apse with three huge windows. A large part of the sculptural architectural decoration and the many statues in

Two panels from the main portal of the Duomo. Made by Pogliaghi, they illustrate scenes from the Life of Mary.

Gian Galeazzo Visconti
(1351-1402)

An ambitious Milanese nobleman, a shrewd politician and a generous patron of the arts, Gian Galeazzo Visconti seized power in 1385 after unscrupulously eliminating his paternal uncle Bernabò. From the very beginning, he attempted to create a modern state, with Milan as its worthy capital and seat of a splendid court; and with a judicious marriage he assured the favor of France. In 1395-1396 Emperor Wenceslas granted him the titles of Duke of Milan and Count of Pavia. He also succeeded in enormously expanding his dominions: over 15 years, he conquered Verona, Vicenza, Padua, Pisa, Siena, Perugia, Assisi, Spoleto, and Bologna. He launched construction of the Duomo of Milan and of the Certosa (Carthusian abbey) of Pavia.

the main body of the Duomo can be attributed to masters from Tuscany, the Veneto region, Campione, France, Germany, Bohemia, and Bourgogne—and most of it dates to the period spanning the 14th and the 15th century. The *facade*, originally conceived in Gothic style but in the 17th century rethought and partly transformed in a Baroque key, was restructured according to the original plan in 1805 by order of Napoleon and was finally completed in Gothic forms.

The **interior** is divided into a soaring nave and four aisles by elegant pillars; with its airy, luminous verticality, it fully recreates the image of that lofty forest that provided the model for the buildings of the pure Gothic. The high cross-vaults and the statues of saints and prophets above the capitals further contribute to refining the already elegant composition. Against the background of the apse, illuminated by the light from the three spectacular stained-glass windows with *Scenes from the Old and New Testaments and the Apocalypse*, beyond the marvelous wooden choir (16th-17th century), there

On the facing page, a view of the soaring Gothic interior of the cathedral.

Right, the funeral monument to Gian Giacomo Medici by Leone Leoni. Bottom, a panel from the left portal of the Duomo.

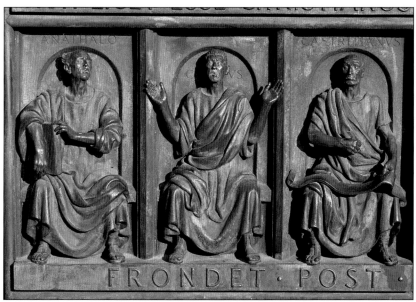

The Holy Nail

In the Duomo of Milan, worshippers venerate a special relic, in a high lantern above the main altar: the Holy Nail. Tradition would have it that this nail, used to crucify Christ, was brought to Italy from Palestine by Saint Helena, mother of Emperor Constantine, in about 330 AD; and that it belonged first to the emperor and later to Saint Ambrose. Since 1461 it has been kept in the Cathedral of Santa Maria Maggiore and is displayed to the faithful every year on 14 September.

Top, a view of the apse from the terrace of the Duomo; below right, the statue of the Madonnina, a well-known symbol of Milan.

Facing page, more images of the Duomo. Top, a window of the apse with a detail of the Last Supper; bottom, the crypt.

The Madonnina
On the highest spire of the cathedral, soaring to 108.50 meters (a height never exceeded by any other of the city's monuments) there sparkles a true symbol of Milan: the statue of the Virgin with its covering of 3900 gold sheets. The statue, universally known as the *Madonnina* (literally, "Our Little Virgin Mary"), was cast in copper in 1774 by Giuseppe Bini to drawings by Giuseppe Perego. Four meters and 16 centimeters tall, this image of the Virgin watches over the city and its inhabitants, surrounded by a crown of smaller spires populated by stars, angels, and saints.

opens the entrance to the **crypt** ordered by Saint Charles Borromeo, whose remains repose here in a crystal reliquary. The Duomo is home to innumerable works of art of inestimable value, from the wooden *crucifix* carried by Saint Charles in procession in 1576 to banish the plague from Milan to the *funeral monument to Gian Giacomo Medici di Marignano*, by Leone Leoni (1563); and from the 14th-century *Pietà with Angels* by a German master to the late 12th-century *Trivulzio Candelabrum* by the bronze-worker Nicholas of Verdun. An idea of the phantasmagoria of precious elements that abound in that true masterpiece of art that is Milan's cathedral is given by its numbers: the cathedral is topped by 135 spires and ornamented with 3159 statues (2245 of which are on the outside) besides the 96 giants on the spouts and the half-figures of the windows; and of course the about 3600 scenes and figures that gleam on the stained-glass windows.

Palazzo Reale

Right on the south side of the Duomo rises the stately complex that is the ancient Palazzo Reale, built on what since 1138 was the site of the *Broletto Vecchio*, the original city hall. The building was later the home of the Visconti family, who softened its appearance, transforming it into the *Corte Ducale*; and later yet, after having been partially demolished—in the late 14th century, to make way for the Duomo—it hosted the Spanish governors and then the city's first permanent civic theater. It was Archduke Ferdinand of Austria who, when he established his residence there, in the 1770's charged the architect Giuseppe Piermarini with the task of making it over as a building in keeping with his position. The facade closest to the Duomo was demolished; the internal facade, until then facing on the courtyard, became the main facade, Neoclassical in style and flanked by two wings that extended to discretely embrace the *Piazzetta Reale*. The interiors were superbly frescoed and decorated by famous Italian and foreign artists: from Traballesi to Knoller and from Albertolli to Appiani and Francesco Hayez. The devastating 1943 bombings inflicted wounds on Palazzo Reale that have never healed: several of the beautiful Neoclassical salons, among which the splendid *Hall of the Caryatids* by Piermarini, and a portion of the frescoes, the mosaics, and the stuccowork were irremediably lost. But despite the devastation, the building—which was later restored—has become the prestigious and logistically perfect venue for temporary exhibitions. It boasts marvelous rooms in what were once the *Royal Apartments*; in the future—when further restoration and enlargement work is completed—it is slated to become a broad-based museum center with creation of the *Museo della Reggia* and the encompassing an expanded *Civico Museo d'Arte Contemporanea* (CIMAC).

Top, a suggestive detail of a room in the Museo del Duomo. Bottom, some of the works in the museum: at the center, the early 15th-century statue of Saint Peter from one of the pilasters of the Duomo.

Museo del Duomo

Since 1953 situated on the ground floor of the Palazzo Reale, in the shadow, we might say, of the cathedral, the Museo del Duomo recounts the history of the construction of this grandiose monument: all the circumstances, the works, the facts that marked five centuries of complex work. Here, we find drawings, models, tapestries, stained glass and works of art, paraments, and other elements—mostly architectural but sculptural as well—subtracted from the Duomo either permanently (for conservation) or temporarily (for restoration). The museum offers its visitors the unique opportunity to learn about the artistic and cultural life of the city during this so long a timespan, with an eye also to the foreign influences (French, Rhenish, Flemish) that so heavily weighed on evolution of Lombard art. And among the innumerable works of art: the *statue of Saint George* (created in 1404 by Giorgio Solari, perhaps in the semblance of Gian Galeazzo Viscon-

Several of the masterpieces in the Museo del Duomo. Left, the cover of the evangelistary *that belonged to Ariberto di Intimiano, a masterpiece of 11th-century goldwork. Above, the keystone of the semi-dome of the apse of the Duomo, depicting God the Father (early 15th century).*

ti), Ariberto's *Crucifix* (1040), the 17th-century *Saint Charles altar frontal*, and the wooden model of the *Madonnina* by Perego (1769). Perhaps most importantly, another wooden model of the Duomo in its entirety, which was more than once modified (as work on the cathedral progressed) between the 16th and 19th centuries; the model is displayed together with the plans for other modifications and single elements that were never actually built.

A detail of the Triptych of the Creation *by Maffiolo da Cremona (late 15th century).*

San Gottardo in Corte

Built as a ducal chapel in 1336 by order of Azzone Visconti, who was later buried in its apse, the church of San Gottardo in Corte is today a unique jewel set in the Palazzo Reale complex thanks to the work conducted in the 18th century by Piermarini, who essentially eliminated the left side and the facade. The Gothic portal on Via Pecorari, now the main entrance to the church, was instead renovated in 1929. All that remains, therefore, of the original 14th-century building is the splendid *apse*, with its cuspidate windows and an upper *loggetta*, and the lovely octagonal bell tower on a square base, built by Francesco Pecorari in brick, with corners in stone and a delicate phantasmagoria of arches, windows with one or two lights, and small columns. The *interior*—a single nave, with a Ionic-columned vestibule—was entirely transformed by Piermarini in accordance with Neoclassical criteria

Notable elements of the church of San Gottardo in Corte include the tall, slender, ethereal bell tower and the Gothic portal.

and decorated with stuccowork by Giocondo Albertolli; it conserves—among other works—a 14th-century fresco by Giotto's school of the *Crucifixion*, originally located at the base of the bell tower, and the *funeral monument to Azzone Visconti*, attributed to Giovanni di Balduccio of Pisa.

Galleria Vittorio Emanuele II

On 7 March 1865, as part of the works for structuring the Piazza del Duomo and in the presence of Vittorio Emanuele II, the first stone was laid for Milan's famous Galleria, which took the king's name; work continued for twelve years. The Galleria is an authentic—and controversial—architectural invention that connects the cathedral area with Piazza della Scala. Besides to the name of the king, it is also inextricably linked to that of its designer, Giuseppe Mengoni, who after its completion fell to his death at less than fifty from a scaffold at the worksite on 30 December 1877, the eve of the inauguration. In memory of the great—and greatly unlucky—architect, a plaque was set in the left column of the towering arch of triumph that gives access to the Galleria from the north side of the Piazza del Duomo. The Galleria takes the form of a cross, with two arms (196 and 105.5 meters) that intersect to form an octagonal *piazza* surmounted by an innovative iron-and-glass *dome* 47 meters high; in 1911, the frescoes (by that time in jeopardy) in the large lunettes were replaced with precious mosaics depicting the four parts of the world: *Europe, Asia, Africa,* and *America.* And with the elegant shops, bookstores, cafés, and restaurants that enliven its already effervescent atmosphere, the Galleria Vittorio Emanuele II, seriously damaged during the 1943 bombings but later carefully restored, has always been—and still is—the favorite meeting-place for the Milanese.

Views and details of the Galleria Vittorio Emanuele, a meeting-place for the Milanese and one of the best-known symbols of the city.

The sober Neoclassical facade of the Teatro alla Scala. This one of the world's most famous opera houses was completed by the architect Giuseppe Piermarini in 1778.

Piazza della Scala

The Galleria Vittorio Emanuele leads into the elegant Piazza della Scala, unfolding around the *monument to Leonardo da Vinci*. Overlooking the square is one of the facades of *Palazzo Marino* (the other, which was originally the front, opens on Piazza San Fedele). Built in 1557 by Galeazzo Alessi for the wealthy Genoese merchant Tommaso Marino, today this *palazzo*, devastated during WW2 and later restored, is Milan's City Hall. It was in this noble home that Marina de Leyva, Marino's niece was born: she was the model for Manzoni's character the Nun of Monza. Facing Palazzo Marino, on the other side of the square, is the unmistakable Teatro alla Scala.

Teatro alla Scala

The Teatro alla Scala, one of the world's most prestigious venues for music as well as Italy's premier opera house, was built by order of Empress Maria Theresa of Austria to plans by Giuseppe Piermarini and was inaugurated on 3 August 1778, two and one-half years after the Teatro Ducale had been destroyed by fire. Its construction was financed by the box-holders of the Teatro Ducale in exchange for permission to build on the land on which rose the church of Santa Maria alla Scala, razed for construction of the new theater but remembered in its name. In counterpoint to the Neoclassical **exterior**, with its sober, measured tones (perhaps justified by the lack of a spacious square before it: the square was opened only in 1858), Piermarini designed a sumptuous **interior** in perfect harmony with the prevailing idea of the *teatro all'italiana*. In the decades following the inauguration, the structure underwent a number of minor modifica-

tions (among which, in 1814, added depth for the stage, obtained by demolishing an adjacent convent on what is now Via Verdi) and significant innovations in the decoration of the interior: in 1807, Giovanni Perego, a top scene designer, was called in to redecorate with new Neoclassical installations, which were further revised and revamped in 1830 by Alessandro Sanquirico. Despite its renown and magnificence, however, the Teatro alla Scala suffered a serious economic crisis in 1897 and was forced to close for a year and reopen under new management. And then, in 1943, the terrible bombing and resulting grave damage. But the theater was rebuilt in short order, an authentic symbol of an entire country's desire for rebirth, and on 11 May 1946 was re-inaugurated with a legendary concert directed by Arturo Toscanini, who had long been the artistic director of the theater. In 1955, the activity of the main structure was flanked by that of the *Piccola Scala*, a smaller theater adjacent to the larger one and reserved for concerts and shows with less demanding scenic requirements. Today—and until 2005—the entire Scala complex is undergoing restoration and restructuring, and all activity has been temporarily relocated to the Teatro degli Arcimboldi.

Images from the history of the Teatro alla Scala. Right, three famous individuals: Olga Preobrajenska, appointed Director of the School of Dance in 1921, Mata-Hari, dancer as well as spy, and Carla Fracci. Bottom, the devastation resulting from the 1943 bombings and a 1946 photo of Arturo Toscanini at the exit of the restored Scala.

The house of the Teatro alla Scala is an elegantly-appointed horseshoe hall with perfect acoustics, 29 meters in length and 21.20 in width, with four orders of boxes (for a total of 155, plus the central "royal box") and two galleries. Total capacity is about 3200.

Images from the history of the Teatro alla Scala. Some of the elegant, colorful posters—many of which are now on exhibit in the adjoining museum—that have announced prestigious performances at the mythical Milanese theater.

The Teatro alla Scala: Present and Future

In late 2001, at the conclusion of the Verdi Centennial season, the Teatro alla Scala closed its doors for ambitious restoration and restructuring work. And thus, since 19 January 2002 and for three seasons in all, the Teatro alla Scala will be operating out of the new **Teatro degli Arcimboldi**, an innovative space, sponsored by the City of Milan, with avant-garde equipment and installations and an audience capacity exceeding that of the Teatro alla Scala by 2400 seats. *Restoration* of the historical theater is mainly concerned with the "monumental" public areas (the facades, house, boxes, galleries, and atriums) while *restructuring* instead concerns the stage area and includes modernizing and adapting the technological elements and systems. The new technical area will cover 1600 square meters, including the stage, the backstage area, a lateral service area, new sectors for preparing the performances, and—thanks to recovery, on the right side, of the former Piccola Scala stage area—it will soon be possible to fully assemble two sets for alternation on stage. The final aim of restoration is thus to create the conditions for alternating performances and titles and so make all the Scala has to offer available to a wider audience.

The Operas

Ever since it was inaugurated, the Teatro alla Scala ha always boasted of its ability to offer, year in and year out, a high-quality playbill featuring international stars and memorable performances. It is therefore no exaggeration to say that this stage has left an indelible mark on music over the last two and one-half centuries: from the Neapolitan opera buffa of Paisiello and Cimarosa to the Neoclassical and Romantic operas (Rossini first of all). And then, of course, there is Mozart, melodrama, Donizetti, the Verists, and Strauss—not to mention the new currents of the early 20th century. While the spectators at the 1778 inauguration heard Salieri's *Europa Riconosciuta*, the unforgettable world premiers at this theater have been many and varied, from Bellini's *Norma* to many works by Verdi (*Nabucco, Aida, Othello, Falstaff*) and Puccini's *Madame Butterfly* and *Turandot*. And as regards the high professional level of the artists, the theater itself has always offered its active, concrete contribution: the theater's historical school of dance was founded in 1813, and 1946 saw the institution of a school for specialist training of young singers. Today, the Teatro alla Scala is host to the **Accademia d'Arti e Mestieri dello Spettacolo**, offering specialization courses for opera singers, orchestra players, and artists working in symphony and opera choruses; there is even a dance department and another conducting laboratories in stagecraft and direction.

The Museum

In 1913, that great Milanese institution that is the Teatro alla Scala decided to dedicate to its own glorious history (and more in general, to the history of opera) the interesting *Museo Teatrale alla Scala* adjacent to the foyer. The museum began with purchase of the collections of the Parisian antique dealer Jules Sambon. Precious assemblies of objects, documents, musical scores, paintings and portraits, original manuscripts, set designs, and instruments—plus a large specialized library—illustrate in detail and with no lack of stimulating anecdotes the artistic events, the famous figures, the triumphs, an other happenings that created the legend of the Scala. Not unsurprisingly, an entire section is dedicated to Giuseppe Verdi. Today (and until 2005) the demanding cycle of restructuring and restoration work on the Teatro alla Scala complex has inevitably involved its museum as well; the collections are still open to the public, however, since they have been transferred to the rooms of *Palazzo Busca*, restored for the occasion, on Piazza Santa Maria delle Grazie across from the Cenacolo Vinciano: the refectory in which Leonardo da Vinci painted his *Last Supper*. It is an extremely elegant venue where the visitor can enjoy the museum's wealth of material ensconced among Neoclassical frescoes and refined stuccowork decoration.

San Fedele

Piazza San Fedele is an elegantly aristocratic corner of Milan that was particularly dear to one of the city's most illustrious sons, Alessandro Manzoni, who lived a stone's throw away for almost 60 years. Overlooking the square is the church of the same name, which boasts a long and noble history. As early as the 9th century the church of Santa Maria in Solario stood on the site; in 1569, when for more than four centuries it had been rededicated to Saint Fidelius, Saint Charles Borromeo decided to transform it into the Baroque church we still see today, on request by the Jesuit order. They made it their headquarters and in an adjoining space built a college, which until 1763 was their professed house in Lombardy. Actually completed only in the 19th century (although with several parts unfinished, like the pediment of the facade and the apse), and restored following the 1943 bombings, San Fedele incorporated the furnishings, the ornaments and vestments, the works of art, and even the 16th-century inlaid *wooden choir* saved from the nearby church of Santa Maria alla Scala when it was demolished, in the 1770's, to make room for the theater of the same name. In San Fedele, in 1771, Mozart directed his *Passion Cantata*, and later on Alessandro Manzoni regularly attended Mass here. The *Madonna dei Torriani*, a 15th-century fresco sheltered in a small chapel, is the sacred image traditionally venerated by the ballerinas of the Scala and for this reason is popularly known as the "Madonna of the Ballerinas" or "of the Artists."

On this page, images of the church of San Fedele: top, the dome and a decorative detail; bottom, the facade and the interior.

Monument to Alessandro Manzoni
Piazza San Fedele, the site from 1872 to 1943 of the Teatro Manzoni (destroyed by the WW2 bombings) and where everything inevitably reminds us of the great writer, born in Milan in 1785, would certainly not be complete without a monument to Alessandro Manzoni. Created in 1883 by the celebrated Milanese sculptor Francesco Barzaghi, the monument was erected near the point of the writer's May 1873 fall down the steps of the church—a fall whose consequences resulted in his death a short time later.

The Betrothed
The Betrothed was Alessandro Manzoni's life work; he had always meditated on the different possibilities for transposing the book's story into literature, in many forms from odes (*Marzo 1821, Cinque Maggio*) to sweeping tragedies (*Il Conte di Carmagnola, Adelchi*). The work behind this novel was arduous: at his attempts to define a story line, a language, and a stylistic dimension suited to the new literary genre, Manzoni worked without pause from 1821 to 1840, producing two preliminary versions (*Fermo e Lucia, Gli sposi promessi*). The final result was a sweeping historical fresco, in which the tangled events in the lives of the betrothed couple create the pretext for Manzoni's masterful narration of the history, the traditions, and the customs of 17th-century Lombardy.

Top, the famous portrait of Manzoni by Francesco Hayez; left, the monument to the great writer in Piazza San Fedele.

The Home of Alessandro Manzoni

A three-story house, graciously decorated in Florentine brick and located right behind Piazza San Fedele, was from 1814 to May 1873 the home of Alessandro Manzoni. Today it is a museum, and everything in the interior is just as it was in the writer's time: the rooms, the furnishings, furniture, and household objects, and the gigantic library—and then original manuscripts, historical documents, and portraits. It was here that the great man of letters studied, lived, and wrote, and received many illustrious guests. And here *The Betrothed* took form. Today, the home and museum is also the headquarters of the *Centro Nazionale di Studi Manzoniani*, founded in 1937, with its collection of all the master's works and critical studies.

The Streets of Milan

Via Monte Napoleone, Via Manzoni, Via della Spiga, Corso Venezia, Via Sant'Andrea—in short, the so-called *Quadrilatero della Moda* (or "Rectangle of Fashion"), a universally-recognized symbol of the luminous and elegant Milan, lively and vibrant, hardworking and inventive: the Milan of the entrepreneurs and the creative cadres. And yet, architecturally speaking, these streets display a precise historical dimension, a sober, discreet 17th-18th century identity. They are lined with the majestic facades of the aristocratic mansions: from the Neoclassical *Palazzo Melzi di Cusano* to *Palazzo Marliani*, by Piermarini, and to *Palazzetto Radice Fossati*, where the poet Carlo Porta lived and died, to name just a few. But today, and in fact since the 1950's, these streets owe their distinction to the luster of the show windows of the up-market shops and boutiques, of the jewelry shops and antique dealers', of the exclusive restaurants, and the characteristic shops dealing in a myriad of tasteful decorating items. We might call the area Milan's elegant drawing-room, its phantasmagoric temple of quality (and outright luxury) shopping, loved and frequented not only by the Milanese but also—and perhaps above all—by foreigners in search of something truly exquisite and exclusive in the very heart of the old city.

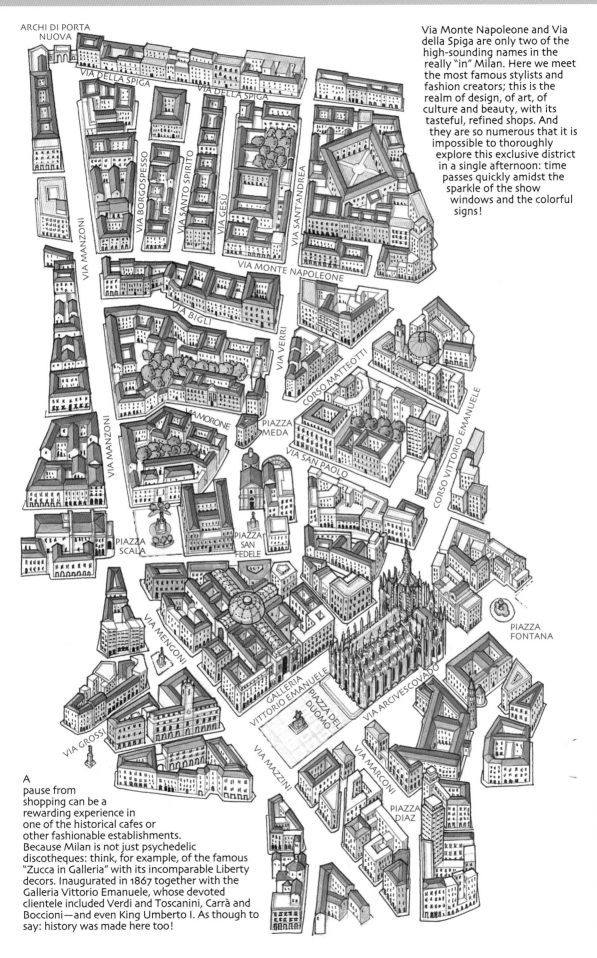

Via Monte Napoleone and Via della Spiga are only two of the high-sounding names in the really "in" Milan. Here we meet the most famous stylists and fashion creators; this is the realm of design, of art, of culture and beauty, with its tasteful, refined shops. And they are so numerous that it is impossible to thoroughly explore this exclusive district in a single afternoon: time passes quickly amidst the sparkle of the show windows and the colorful signs!

ARCHI DI PORTA NUOVA

VIA DELLA SPIGA

VIA DELLA SPIGA

VIA BORGOSPESSO

VIA SANTO SPIRITO

VIA GESÙ

VIA SANT'ANDREA

VIA MANZONI

VIA MONTE NAPOLEONE

VIA BIGLI

VIA VERRI

CORSO MATTEOTTI

CORSO VITTORIO EMANUELE

VIA MANZONI

VIAMORONE

PIAZZA MEDA

VIA SAN PAOLO

PIAZZA SCALA

PIAZZA SAN FEDELE

PIAZZA FONTANA

VIA MENGONI

GALLERIA VITTORIO EMANUELE

PIAZZA DEL DUOMO

VIA ARCIVESCOVADO

VIA GROSSI

VIA MAZZINI

VIA MARCONI

PIAZZA DIAZ

A pause from shopping can be a rewarding experience in one of the historical cafes or other fashionable establishments. Because Milan is not just psychedelic discotheques: think, for example, of the famous "Zucca in Galleria" with its incomparable Liberty decors. Inaugurated in 1867 together with the Galleria Vittorio Emanuele, whose devoted clientele included Verdi and Toscanini, Carrà and Boccioni—and even King Umberto I. As though to say: history was made here too!

Museo Poldi Pezzoli

Gian Giacomo Poldi Pezzoli (1822-1879), a Milanese nobleman, was the son of Giuseppe and his wife Rosa Trivulzio, daughter of one of the most polished and highly aristocratic families of Neoclassical Milan, patrons of the arts and letters. There is no doubt that it was his mother's teaching that led Gian Giacomo, who lost his father at the age of 11 years, to develop that intense passion that soon induced him to place his immense financial resources at the service of his lifelong activity as a collector of paintings, weapons and armor, glass, jewels, ceramics, fabrics, and furniture: between 1850 and his death in 1879, the nobleman put together a true gallery of extraordinary artistic masterpieces that he arranged personally in his home, with its rooms decorated to his order in different styles of the past to best harmonize with objects datable to various periods (among these spaces, the armory, the Sala Nera, the Salone Dantesco, the Salone Dorato, and the elegant entrance staircase are particularly famous): in short, a home that was bit by bit transformed into a *museum* to all effects. And indeed the entire building in Via Manzoni, at the death of its owner, was donated to the City of Milan on condition that it be incorporated as a *Fondazione Artistica* (Foundation for the Arts) for the enjoyment and benefit of the public and that the dedicated collector's arrangement of the rooms not be in any way modified. Thus, this extraordinary institution (which became the model for many later museum-homes), famous for the works it contains (from ancient to 19th-century art, with paintings by Italian masters of outstanding fame, from Botticelli to Piero della Francesca, from Mantegna to Pollaiolo, from Canaletto to Tiepolo), is still today a faithful mirror of the romantic vision of art prevalent among the collectors of the latter half of the 19th century. The collections are arranged by qualitative and artistic as well as historical criteria. The 1943 bombing literally devastated the museum: the roofs, the skylights, and the stuccowork col-

Sandro Botticelli,
Lamentation over the Dead Christ

We still do not now exactly how this tempera on wood ended up in Gian Giacomo Poldi Pezzoli's collection: it may be that altarpiece, in the church of Santa Maria Maggiore in Florence, defined as "very beautiful" by Vasari. According to some critics, the work was commissioned of Botticelli by Donato di Antonio Cioli, an illuminator of manuscripts for that church. Painted in 1495, the panel is attributable to Botticelli's later period, when he lived with his brother Simon, an ardent *piagnone* or follower of Savonarola. Even though Vasari defined Botticelli as being "a strong partisan of that sect," in truth the artist was not a true follower: he limited himself to expressing, at the stylistic level, the profound sense of moral disquiet that derived from the ascetic preaching of the Dominican friar. This painting is a clear example: it lacks the sinuous, graceful line of the earlier paintings; here, instead, these qualities give way to a pyramidal structure and the pronounced sentimentalism expressed in the gestures of the figures and the facial expressions. The body of Christ that cuts across the scene breaks the verticality of the composition: a lifeless corpse, which none of those present can bring himself to regard.

Antonio del Pollaiolo,
Portrait of a Young Woman Girl

A masterpiece by the great Florentine painter, dated about 1470, this elegant and refined portrait depicts the proud, determined profile of a lovely young woman on whose golden hair the light sublimely plays and reflects. Against the background of a blue sky with clouds, the face of the noble figure stands out cleanly and in rigorously full profile, according to the canons of ancient portraiture, while the bust is turned slightly, in a three-quarter view. The elaborate hairstyle, the rich clothing, and the precious jewels are unequivocal testimony to the high social standing of the young woman, which an ancient inscription on the back of the panel identified as the wife of the well-to-do Florentine banker Giovanni de' Bardi.

Andrea Mantegna, *Virgin with Child*

Halfway through the 15th century there occurred, in northern Italy, a very important event for art history: the Florentine sculptor Donatello came to Padua, and met Andrea Mantegna. Their encounter marked the beginning of a fundamental phase in the Venetian painter's artistic career. This *Virgin with Child* acquired by Poldi Pezzoli in 1856 is a masterpiece: not only of Mantegna's production but of the entire history of art as well. It is from Donatello's sculpture that the solid plasticity of Mantegna's painting derives; the Virgin is one with her small, sleeping Son, held in a strong yet tender embrace. The two figures run the one into the other, wrapped by the Virgin's mantle into a single compact form, an exquisite expression of gentle intimacy and the unique emotion felt by a mother watching over and protecting her child.

Lorenzo Bartolini, *Faith in God*

The masterful Italian sculptor from the early 1800's Lorenzo Bartolini created this polished work in marble in 1835. The smooth surfaces of the carefully-chosen material, the naturalness of the delicate nude forms of the lovely girl, caught in a state of profound religious transport, and the extreme fluidity of the lines elegantly characterize this harmonious, ecstatic sculpture. The result is an expression that enthralls the viewer, projecting emotions of extraordinary intensity, while the evident references to Renaissance style succeed in becoming a privileged vehicle for transmitting profound and educational moral concepts.

lapsed, the wooden elements burned, the splendid decorations were irreparably damaged—all that was saved were the works previously transferred, with remarkable foresight, to safer places. After the war the entire building was accurately restored and the museum reopened on 3 December 1951.
Over the years, the original nucleus of collections have been augmented by donations from private collectors for a total of about a thousand pieces added in the last 50 years. Today, the museum also organizes temporary exhibits, often linked to the history of collecting.

Walls and Gates

Ever since Milan first began to take on the look of a city it has been protected by a powerful circle of walls; periodically, as the city center expanded and it needs changed, the circle was replaced by more extensive ones, until the majestic *Spanish walls* were built in the 16th century. Time passed and times changed, however, and slowly this fortified perimeter lost any *raison d'être*. And yet in places there still remain proud reminders of the ancient bastions: above all, the huge *gates* that now straddle the city's streets but that for so long were the transit points for goods and people entering and exiting Milan. Only two may be said to have been truly monumental: *Porta Romana* (the oldest, dating to 1596, through which the nobility of Milan and illustrious personages traditionally passed) and *Porta Orientale* (1787). Another five were, in any case, of no small importance: *Porta Ticinese, Porta Vercellina, Porta Volta, Porta Comasina,* and *Porta Nuova.* The latter two gates were built only in the 19th century, when the bastions were already being transformed into innocuous tree-lined boulevards.

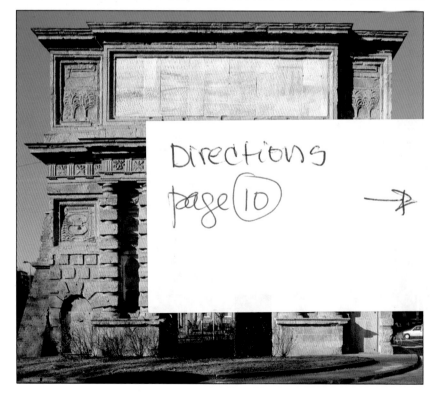

City gates of Milan: from the top, the Neoclassical Porta Nuova, Porta Garibaldi, and Porta Romana; below, Porta Ticinese.

Directions
page (10)
→

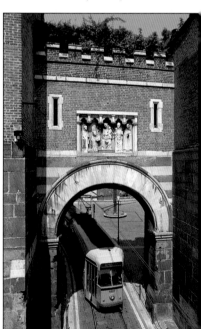

Castello Sforzesco

Together with the Duomo, the Castello Sforzesco is undoubtedly the most authentic and well-loved symbol of Milan. The original nucleus was built by order of Galeazzo II Visconti between 1360 and 1370 as a defensive bulwark; against the medieval city walls, it incorporated the ancient Porta Giovia. It was originally built on a square plan extending to 180 meters per side and was protected by four corner towers. Filippo Maria Visconti was the first to transform the fort (which over the years had been further strengthened) into a residence; at the same time, he also set out the park that opened to the north of the well-served citadel. But when he died in 1447 with no male heirs, the Milanese proclaimed the Republic and neither did they hesitate to raze the castle, an unwieldy symbol of Visconti power, to the ground. Three years later, when he entered Milan as the city's new *signore*, Francesco Sforza, able leader of troops and above all the son-in-law of Filippo Maria Visconti for having married his only

The beautiful Visconti family coat-of-arms. Bottom, an aerial view of the Castello Sforzesco.

daughter, the illegitimate Bianca Maria, immediately began reconstruction of the forbidding fortification. He made use of foundations of the Visconti castle but at the same time attempted to mitigate the severity of the forms with such additions as the round towers designed by the military architect Bartolomeo Gadio and Filarete's majestic 70-meter tower at the entrance. As time went on, however, and the Sforza's hold was consolidated, the lords of Milan began to feel the need for a residence that was not only fortified and secure but also elegant and refined: a statelier home more representative of their station and able to provide the comforts demanded by the functions a princely family is called to perform. Thus, in 1446, Francesco's son Galeazzo Maria Sforza ordered that in the very heart of the castle there be constructed the great and nobly porticoed Corte Ducale flanked by the squared-off stronghold known as *La Fortezza*. Over it rises the soaring, 36-meter Torre di Bona, called thus because it was or-

The Castello Sforzesco

Built in the mid-14th century in the heart of the old city by the Visconti family and many times enlarged and strengthened until assuming both the form and functions of a true fortress, the majestic Castello Sforzesco, for a long time also the seat of a splendid court, is today one of the best-loved and best-known symbols of Milan, historical and otherwise.

Porta del Barco

Loggia Galeaz. Maria

Cortile della Rocchetta

Torre Castellana

Rivellino di Porta Vercellina

Torre di Bona di Savoia

Porta Santo Spirito

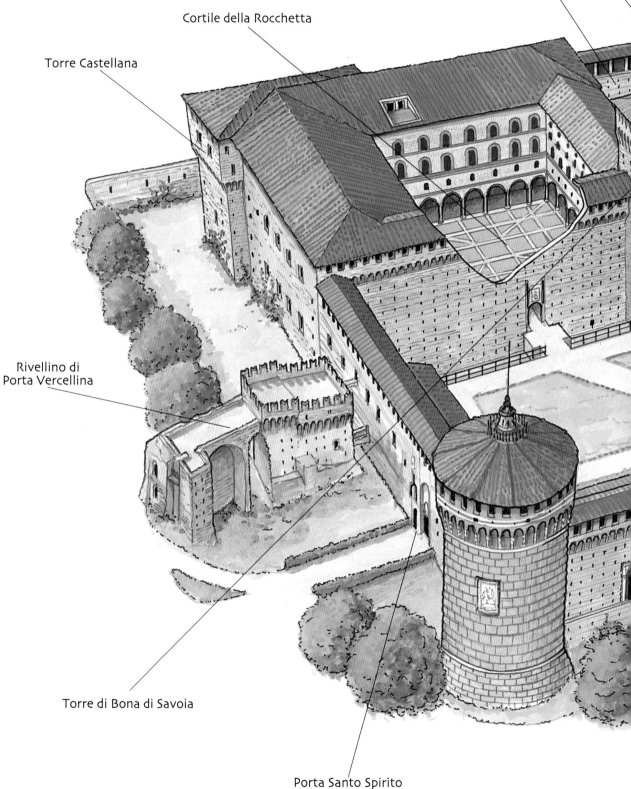

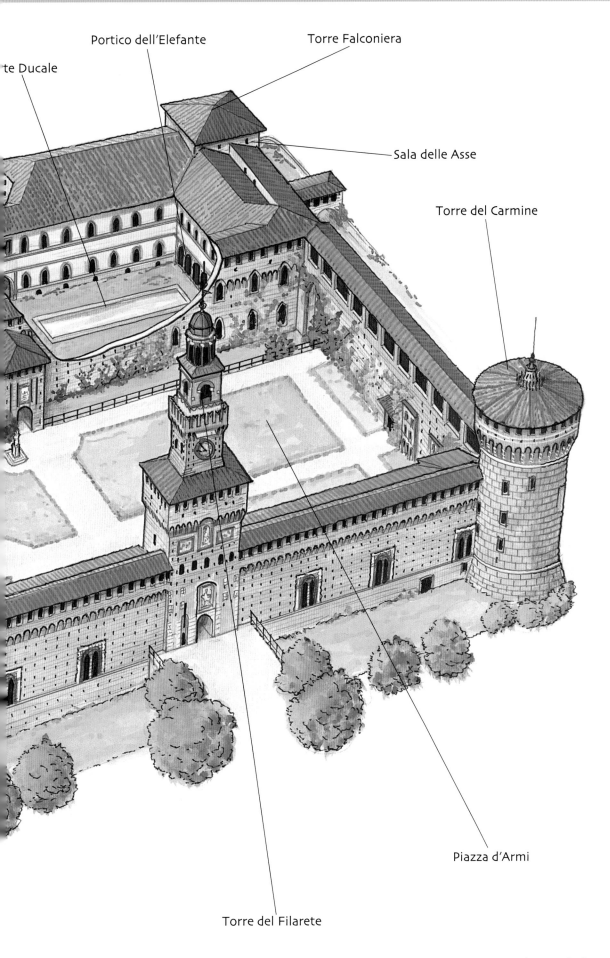

Portico dell'Elefante

Torre Falconiera

te Ducale

Sala delle Asse

Torre del Carmine

Piazza d'Armi

Torre del Filarete

dered by Bona di Savoia, the wife and later widow of Galeazzo Maria. Then it was the turn of Ludovico il Moro ("the Moor") to continue the demanding work of embellishing the Castello—and he called in the best artists of the time, from Donato Bramante to Leonardo da Vinci. Thus, in the last two decades of the 15th century the Castello gained an addition in the form of a small but especially lovely wing known as the *Ponticella*, facing out on the external moat, but also a flowering garden of splendid frescoes, like those in the *Sala delle Asse*. With the start of French rule in 1499, and the series of sieges and sacks and the ravages of war, the star of the Castello Sforzesco seemed irremediably doomed to set. A sign of the times was had when the Torre del Filarete, at the time a munitions dump, exploded on 23 June 1521. Five years later the Spanish, as new rulers of Milan, lost little time in reinforcing the complex. They later girded it (from 1560 onward) with a formidable star-shaped fortification that made it practically impossible to breach; by the early 1600's the fortifications had acquired a total of 12 points thanks to insertion of six detached demilunes. This spectacular structure was left untouched by the Austrians, who for much of the 18th century used the Castello as a military base. Brought under siege by Napoleon's troops in 1796, it was later expunged and severely damaged (the Milanese themselves saw to partially demolishing the corner towers and even mutilated the Sforza coats-of-arms), and was deprived of its outer star-shaped fortifications. The central nucleus, the Castello proper, was placed at the disposition of the troops and the Corte Ducale area was used as stabling facilities. All around, meanwhile, the plan for the Bonaparte Forum began to take shape. Again occupied by the Austrians from 1814 onward, the castle was attacked by the population in 1848 at the time of the Five Days of Milan; it nevertheless continued to host the Imperial garrisons until 1859—despite its having been even further mutilated and its architectural integrity placed in severe jeopardy. Only following Italian unification and the acquisition of

Top, the castle moat with the passage to the Porta del Barco. Bottom, the statue of Garibaldi in front of the Torre del Filarete; left and on the facing page, two images of the lovely tower.

the entire complex by the City of Milan could the Castello again hope to aspire to a brilliance worthy of its long history—but even then, there were those who, due to its extremely poor conditions, repeatedly and unrepentingly suggested and promoted its complete demolition. The lengthy, painstaking restoration work began in 1893; much of the merit for the result is due to the zealous commitment of the architect Luca Beltrami, who demolished what remained of the exterior fortifications but also rebuilt the towers, reopened the moat and fosses, and restored the battlements and the trussed roofs. The *Rocchetta* and the *Torre di Bona* reacquired their original looks. Even the *Torre del Filarete*, with its great *clock* and the *statue of Saint Ambrose*, was rebuilt identical to the original and inaugurated in 1904.

Some views of the interior of the Castello Sforzesco: top, Roman ruins in the Piazza d'Armi; center, the Cortile della Rocchetta; bottom, the Corte Ducale with at its far end the Portico dell'Elefante, so-called after the figure of a pachyderm once frescoed on its wall.

With the 20th century, the Castello Sforzesco was finally returned intact to the city, which gave the premises over to museums, libraries, and cultural institutions, so guaranteeing to it a public function of especial prestige—as, we might say, was only its due.

Today, the great complex, damaged in the bombings of 1943 and again restored, once again presents a substantial uniformity of composition among the facade, the sides, and the rear facade (where the *Torre Castellana* and the *Torre Falconiera* rise), and incorporates three courtyards. The largest, reached through the Torre del Filarete—flanked at the extremities of the wall by the *Torrione dei Carmini* and the *Torrione di Santo Spirito*, both 31 meters in height—is the *Piazza d'Armi* behind which the Torre di Bona rises. Beyond are smaller courts: the elegant *Corte Ducale* with the Renaissance *Portico dell'Elefante* and the gracious *Loggia di Galeazzo Maria*, both 15th-century works by Ferrini, and the *Cortile della Rocchetta*, protected by the stronghold of the same name and with porticoes on three sides, one by Benedetto Ferrini, one by Filarete, and one by Bernardino da Corte. The interiors also preserve unaltered the elegance of the scintillating Sforza period, with splendid frescoes and elegant decorations—above all in the rooms that wind around the Corte Ducale but also in those that look out on the Cortile della Rocchetta.

Castello Sforzesco Museums

Museum of Ancient Art

The museum counts 15 rooms on the ground floor of the Corte Ducale, with access from the Pusterla dei Fabbri arch. The *first room* is host to sculptures, frescoes, and mosaics from the 4th to the 11th century notable among the most ancient sculptures is the *head* traditionally said to represent Empress Theodora. *Room 2*, decorated during Spanish rule with coats-of-arms and bouquets of flowers, is dedicated to sculpture in Milan and Lombardy, from the Romanesque to the Gothic. Much space is reserved for the works produced by the skilled workmen from the Campione area who were active in Italy and northern Europe from the second half of the 12th century to the end of the 14th. Bonino da Campione is the author of the masterpiece in the center of the room, the *sepulchral monument to Bernabò Visconti*, lord of Milan from 1354 to 1385, which stands alongside another work of the Campionese school, the monument to *his wife Regina Della Scala*. *Room 3* contains further examples of the art of Campione and Lombardy and fine examples of Tuscan sculpture, in-

Among the prestigious works in the Ancient Art and Sculpture Collections are the funeral monument to Gastone de Foix, by Bambaja (1516-1525; left, a detail) and the 12th-century bas-relief of a sacred procession, from the church of Santa Maria Beltrade (below).

Again in the Ancient Art and Sculpture Collections, this marvelous head of Empress Theodora, a noble example of Byzantine art dating to the 6th century.

cluding the entire complex of statues by Giovanni di Balduccio and his workshop, from the tabernacles of Porta Orientale and Porta Ticinese. The frescoed coat-of-arms of the king of Spain Philip II and his wife Maria Tudor, a rare testimonial to the Spanish presence in the Castello, overshadows the exhibits in *Room 4* of important architectural and decorative fragments from the lost facade of the church of Santa Maria di Brera, now absorbed into the fabric of the palazzo. After *Room 5*, with interesting 14th- and 15th-century works on religious themes, come *Rooms 6* and *7*, devoted to the most important events in the history of Milan. In the first of these two rooms, among other works, is the *bell of Broletto*, a symbol of the city, and some of the capitals sculpted in the 12th century to adorn Porta Romana. The celebration of the glories of Milan continues into *Room 7*, called the *Sala del Gonfalone* because it contains the gonfalon or standard of Milan created in 1565 by the embroiderers Scipione Delfinone and Camillo Pusterla to patterns by Giuseppe Meda. *Room 8*, also called the *Sala delle Asse*, is famous because it recalls the time spent in Milan by Leonardo da Vinci, who frescoed the ceiling with a false pergola of the tightly-interwoven, flowered boughs of 16 trees laced with a golden rope. The two adjoining small rooms are called *"Negre"* because it is said that it was here that Ludovico il Moro retired while mourning his wife Beatrice, who died in 1497. Next are the *Sala dei Ducali* and the *Cappella Ducale*, both built by order of Galeazzo Maria Sforza: on exhibit here are 15th-century works of sculpture of the Lombard and northern Italian schools. Especially important is the *bas-relief of episodes from the life of Saint Sigismund* by the Florentine Agostino di Duccio. Fine sculptures from the Lombard Renaissance are exhibited in *Room 13*, or the *Sala delle Colombine*, decorated in dark red and with the eye-catching heraldic device of the dove in the golden-rayed sun with the motto *"a bon droit."* The last two

Rondanini Pietà

When Michelangelo died in the Roman home of Macel de' Corvi, on 18 February 1564, he had not completed the *Pietà* sculptural group that was to have been set on his tomb. In fact, only six days before his death the artist had partially modified the proportions of the statues, exasperating that sense of plastic power that is so evident in the other *Pietà* in the cathedral of Florence. In this *Pietà* in Milan, Michelangelo changed the position of the Virgin's head, turning it centerward, and accentuated the contrast between the smoothed and roughed surfaces, chiseling Christ's chest. Vasari tells us that Michelangelo was rarely content with his work in the field of sculpture, and that "... *come gli aveva scoperto una figura, e conosciutovi un minimo che d'errore, lo lasciava stare, e correva a manimettere un altro marmo*" ("... as he uncovered a figure and discovered in it even a minimum of error, he left it and ran to work on other marble"). Whether Michelangelo had some second thoughts about this *Pietà*, or simply felt his end was drawing near, an intensely dramatic sense explodes from the elongated, spectral forms of the two figures and in the extreme gesture of the Virgin who seems to want to call back her son in a last desperate embrace. In his old age, the artist has achieved his aim: to annul the form, too human and terrestrial, and to exalt the soul. As Georg Simmel wrote in his perceptive essay on Michelangelo, there was no longer matter that the soul must oppose.

with the motto "*a bon droit.*" The last two rooms are the *Sala Verde*, or *Sala delle Armi*, and the *Sala degli Scarlioni*. In the first of these are various types of weapons; notable, for its great historical importance, is Radetsky's parade saber. In the second—called thus after the white and red frescoes with zigzag motifs that the Sforza defined "*a scaglioni*" or "*a scarlioni*"—are two of the museum's most important works: the *funeral monument to Gaston de Foix*, a masterpiece by Bambaja, and the *Rondanini Pietà* by Michelangelo.

Museum of Musical Instruments and Applied Arts Collections

These two important collections are housed on the first and second floors of the Rocchetta. In the Sala della Balla we find the celebrated *Arazzi dei Mesi*, also known as the *Trivulzio Tapestries*, woven to drawings by Bramantino. In the following rooms, the rich collection of musical instruments, including 16th- and 17th-century plucked, and bowed string instruments, and wind instruments, Hans Ruckers' double virginal, a guitar with five tiers of strings, a mid-16th century Venetian harpsichord, and an ivory oboe dated 1722. The Applied Arts Collections also count works of great value: objects in gold, like the *Voghera monstrance* in the form of a Gothic templet, ivories dating to the 4th-18th century (extremely beautiful, the *Trivulzio plaque* portraying the family of Emperor Otto), enameled pieces from Limoges, and many scientific instruments. There are also works in wrought iron, glass, majolica and porcelain, from the Middle Ages to the 19th century, including pieces from the factories of Meissen, Vienna, and Capodimonte, as well as the Ginori works near Florence.

Furniture Collections and Pinacoteca

Among the most beautiful and significant of the objects in the *collection of furniture and wooden decoration* on the first floor of the Corte Ducale are those crafted by Giuseppe Maggiolini in the Neo-classical period. The *Pinacoteca del Castello Sforzesco* is instead located in the Torre Falconiera; here, arranged in chronological order, are 14th- to 18th-century paintings, including masterpieces by Mantegna, Correggio, Filippo Lippi, and Antonello da Messina. The most important section of the gallery is that with paintings of the Lombard school: from works by Foppa, Bergognone, and Bramantino, through the followers of Leonardo, to the works of Procaccini (*The Martyrdom of Saint Sebastian*), Cerano, and Morazzone. *Room 26* is completely given over to portraits, with paintings by Correggio, Andrea Solario, Giovanni Bellini, Lotto (*Portrait of a Young Man with a Book*), Romanino, Titian, Tintoretto, Bronzino, and Van Dyck (*Portrait of Henriette Marie of France*).

Applied Arts Collections: an astrolabe with Latin planisphere, from the 14th century.

Prehistoric Museum

The collections of this interesting museum are arranged in the cellar of the Rocchetta and the Sala Viscontea, in three sections: the Neolithic, the Bronze Age, and the Iron Age. The materials of the Lagozza culture of Besnate (near Varese) fall into the first of these periods; there are a great number of chipped, polished stone tools from many sites in northern Italy, illustrating stone-dressing from the 6th to the 4th millennium BC. The Bronze Age exhibit includes a broad range of terracotta vases modeled by hand in various forms and decorated with geometrical motifs. A showcase contains bronze products like arrowheads, hairpins, and axe-heads; the various stages in bronze- horn- and woodworking are copiously exemplified. The last of the Bronze Age exhibits shows materials relative to the Scamozzina and Canegrate cultures, in which cremation became a common funerary rite. Finally we come to the Iron Age exhibits: the Protogolasecca culture (12th to 10th century BC) with the furnishings of the warrior's tomb of Sesto Calende, dated to the 7th century BC and discovered in 1867; and Tomb 10 of Albate and the tomb of Trezzo sull'Adda, both of which contained extraordinary numbers of ornaments and valuable objects. The visit to the museum ends with the exhibit of materials from the culture of La Tène, which appeared in northern Italy in the late 5th century BC and called thus for the name of a Swiss archaeological site on the Lake of Neuchâtel.

The Ancient Art and Sculpture Collections are home to this elaborate 12th-century Telamon *attributed to Wiligelmo.*

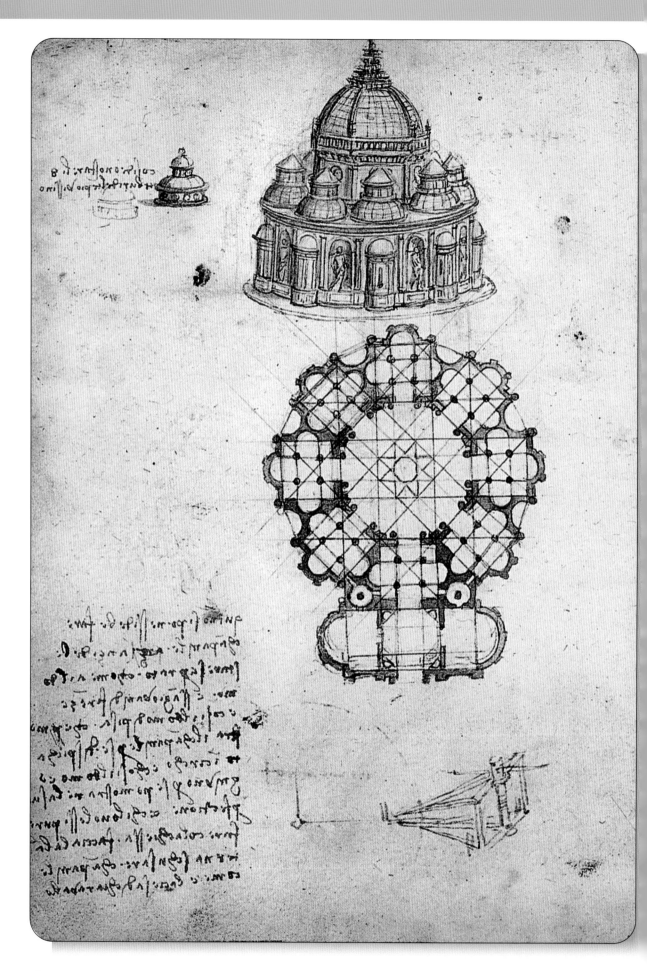

THE IDEAL CITY

If someone today—engineer, town planner, or architect—wanted to a plan for an ideal futuristic city, he would find it hidden in Leonardo's Codices. In a letter to Ludovico il Moro, Duke of Milan, Leonardo describes, imagines, dreams a "new city" with public and private buildings, with open green spaces and canals: a city that is a perfect fusion of man and the environment, built in harmony with nature. Leonardo imagined a city constructed near a river, with eternally clean waters always evenly-flowing. A city on two levels—streets above the houses for pedestrian use only, other thoroughfares at ground level for commercial traffic—and with an underground drainage system. *"Per le strade alte no' de' andare carri nè altre simili cose, anzi sia solamente per le gentili òmini; per le basse deono andare i carri o l'altre some a l'uso e comodità del popolo [...]; per le vie socteranee si de' votare destri, stalle e simili cose fetide"* ("Carriages and other similar things must not go on the high streets, but rather only gentlefolk; on the lower must go the wagons and other carriers for the use and convenience of the populace . . . the underground ways must be used for stables and oth-

Leonardo

An eclectic and extremely talented figure with extraordinary qualities as a painter, architect, scientist, and writer, Leonardo di ser Piero was born in Vinci on 15 April 1452. From childhood onward, this illegitimate son of a wealthy notary displayed extraordinary curiosity as well as an out-of-the-ordinary bent for learning and scientific thought. He acquired his artistic training in the *bottega* of Andrea Verrocchio in Florence. Later, taken under the wing of Lorenzo il Magnifico, the young Leonardo was early on called to give proof of his genius at the foremost courts and capitals of the age. In 1482 he was in Milan, at the court of the Sforza family; in 1499 in Venice; and in 1503 in Florence—and then Rome, Milan again, and finally France, where he was invited by King Francis I in 1503. Leonardo died in Amboise, France, on 2 May 1519. As a painter, he invented the sfumato technique that highlights the delicate contrasts of light and shadow that are so clearly in evidence in the *Last Supper*. But he was also responsible for an incredible quantity of basic and innovative research in the fields of mechanics, anatomy, optics, chemistry, geology, astronomy, and many sectors of architecture, above all military.

er dirty things . . ."). And then canals and fountains, vast squares and gardens, tall, majestic buildings with broad closed courtyards. This innovative humanistic concept never found practical application, since Leonardo never obtained from Ludovico that "authority" that would have permitted him to build the "five thousand houses with thirty thousand dwellings" called for by his extraordinary plan. But in its utopian beauty, Leonardo's ideal city is still perfect, possible, and today, perhaps, could actually be built.

Studies for a central-plan church, for various mechanisms, and for a machine for canal drainage. The Castello Sforzesco library provides precious testimony to Leonardo's genius in the Codex Trivulzianus.

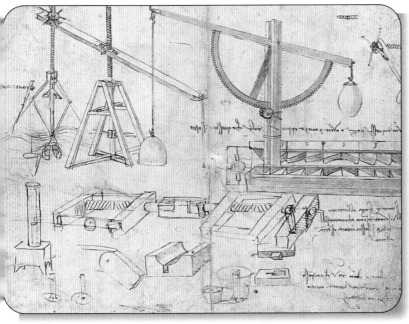

Parco Sempione

Exiting the Castello Sforzesco through the *Porta del Barco* at the center of the front facade of the fortress, the first thing we see is the green prospect of the huge, luxuriant Parco del Sempione with its 47 hectares: the largest of the parks in the city cen-ter and much cherished the Milanese people. Creat-ed in 1893 by the architect Emilio Alemagna on site of what in the 15th century was the enormous ducal garden (or "*Barcho*"), the park actually owes its present-day existence to the widespread crisis that at the time plagued Milan's building industry and provided the needed impetus. The park was conceived as a huge English garden, with wide,

Top left, Giorgio De Chirico's Bagni Misteriosi*; top right, the Torre Branca; bottom, the iron-and-concrete Anfiteatro.*

curving, crossing boulevards, pleasant stands of trees, and a large central lawn; it is planted to offer magnificent plays of perspective on the Castello Sforzesco and the Arco della Pace, at its two extremities. At the center of the lawn is the lake, from which two watercourses lead out. One is crossed by the *Ponte delle Sirenette*, moved here from the city's canals in 1830: its name derives from the four *statues of Sirens* that adorn it, works in cast iron by the sculptor Tettamanti. Also at the center of the park is De Chirico's *Fontana Metafisica* or *Bagni Misteriosi* ("Metaphysical Fountain" or "Mysterious Baths") and also *Monte Tordo*, a rise on which stands the *Monument to Napoleon III* by Francesco Barzaghi.

The Palazzo dell'Arte, permanent home of the Triennale d'Arte Decorativa.

Palazzo dell'Arte

On the west side of Parco Sempione, the Palazzo dell'Arte built in 1933 by Giovanni Muzio is the permanent home of the Triennale d'Arte Decorativa di Milano ("Triennial Exhibition of Decorative Art of Milan"). The Palazzo is flanked by the *Torre del Parco*, once known as the *Torre Littoria*; it is 109 meters in height and was built of steel pipes in 1932 to plans by Cesare Chiodi, Giò Ponti, and Ettore Ferrari. On a three-yearly basis, the *Triennale d'Arte Decorativa*, established in 1923, organizes a multifaceted international exhibition dedicated to modern architecture and to the most widely-varied—but all high quality—artistic/industrial activities; it also features interesting cultural initiatives and is concretely committed to experimentation and research. In the intervals between one edition and the next, the Palazzo dell'Arte hosts temporary exhibits and special attractions.

A view of Parco Sempione with the Arco della Pace in the background.

Arco della Pace

The Arco della Pace or Arch of Peace was begun in 1807 to plans by the marquis Luigi Cagnola. Napoleon Bonaparte urged its construction: he exhorted the Milan City Council to erect an Arch of Triumph suitable for directing the gaze toward Paris, a new entrance from which the emperor could enjoy solemn access to the city. But, due to various historical/political events, it was completed

only in 1838; when it was inaugurated in September of that year it was by a different emperor, Ferdinand I Hapsburg, who dedicated it to another Hapsburg, Francis I, and to celebrating the peace achieved in Europe in 1815. When the Savoia family later rose to power, the banner inscriptions were replaced and the arch was rededicated to the new unified Italy. The arch, a sober creation in Neoclassical style, with a structure in granite and marble facings, soars to 25 meters' height; it features three arches, the center one much wider than the other two. Crowned as it is by the majestic *Chariot of Peace*, a work in bronze by Abbondio Sangiorgio, by Giovanni Putti's *Mounted Victories* and by the representations of the four rivers of Lombardy and Veneto (*Po, Ticino, Adige,* and *Tagliamento*), this majestic monument is notable for these elements and the rest of its elaborate decoration, consisting of *reliefs* inspired by episodes from the Restoration.

Left, a bas-relief from the Arco della Pace topped by the bronze Chariot of Peace (bottom right), and a panoramic view of the arch with the two small buildings at the sides (bottom left).

Acquario Civico

Founded in 1906 in the very heart of Parco Sempione by the Società Lombarda per la Pesca e l'Acquicoltura, which later donated it to the City of Milan, the Acquario Civico (aquarium) is one of the world's oldest institutions of this type. One of the most distinctive buildings in the aquarium complex (destroyed in 1943, rebuilt, fitted with state-of-the-art equipment, and reopened in 1963) is in gracious *Liberty* style with beautiful period decoration on its *facades* (tondi with fish, crustaceans—including lobsters—and turtles, polychrome majolica fasciae, and a statue of Neptune by Oreste Labò). From the very beginning dedicated to teaching activities and exhibits, the Acquario Civico contains 36 tanks reconstructing the environments populated by about 100 species of aquatic organisms: from the riverside walk, with its fresh-water creatures, to various Mediterranean habitats like the rocky and sandy coasts, to the waters of Amazon and the coral reefs. A special section is reserved for the wetlands typical of the Po river valley; a special terrarium shows off numerous species of amphibians. Another interesting attraction is the well-stocked library, while the adjacent *Stazione Idrobiologica* (hydrobiological station) is the center for scientific research centering on the fields of fresh- and salt-water biology and ecology.

Arena

The great Arena or Civic Stadium rises almost at the end of the Parco Sempione, on the east side just a short way from the aquarium. It is elliptical in form (measuring 238 by 116 meters) and Neoclassical in style—an interesting creation by Luigi Canonica dating to 1806 and officially inaugurated the following year in the presence of Napoleon. In truth, the first modern Arena was built in 1803, in wood, to plans by Andrea Appiani, who undoubtedly took his inspiration from the tiered amphitheater of classical antiquity, access to which was through the gates opening at the four sides. Of greatest interest among these, in the case of the Arena as it currently stands, is the enormous *Porta Trionfale*, a true arch of triumph. Once the venue for naumachiae and chariot races, the great stadium today hosts sports contests and other events.

From the top, the statue of Neptune at the entrance to the Acquario Civico and the facade of the Arena Civica.

Next page, the historical center of Milan seen from the Castello Sforzesco.

Palazzo Litta

Not far from the Castello Sforzesco is the elegant **Corso Magenta**, a broad thoroughfare lined by noble, austere buildings, mute witnesses to a Milan that even under foreign domination was more than able accumulate wealth and power. One of the most outstanding, in all its magnificence, is the splendid Palazzo Litta, more precisely denominated Arese Borromeo Litta. The palazzo was built for Count Bartolomeo Arese, a high dignitary of the Spanish court and from 1660 onward President of the Milan Senate. Construction began in 1648 on what was at the time Corso di Porta Vercellina, to plans by the architect Francesco Richini. The annexes and gardens, which ran almost to the Castello, were maintained until the palaces of the Bonaparte Forum were raised. Already famous for the legendary receptions held by Count Arese, for the illustrious guests it hosted, and for the rich art collections it housed, it was later embellished with the magnificent *grand staircase* added by Giuseppe Merli in about 1740 and the Baroque *facade* designed by Bartolomeo Bolla (1752-1763). Later yet were added the splendid *decorations* with which Knoller and Gerli graced the halls, from the *Salotto Rosso* to the *Salone degli Specchi* and the *Salotto della Duchessa*. In the meantime, the mansion was the object of complex questions of inheritance and succession, and all the more so because Count Bartolomeo left only two daughters who married, respectively, Count Renato Borromeo and Count Fabio Visconti. The building was purchased by the State Railways in 1874 and became the seat of the Departmental Headquarters. Today, Palazzo Litta is once again a city cultural heritage and even its ancient (and now restructured, enlarged, and modernized) *theater*, originally enjoyed by the noble family and their guests alone, is open to the public.

Two details of Palazzo Litta: top, the Litta family coat-of-arms, bottom, the entrance portal to the mansion.

Receptions at Palazzo Litta
For centuries, the mansion of Count Arese was a renowned venue for magnificent receptions and parties, intoned with the prestige and power of its founder and his descendents. The most famous has always been that organized in 1649 during Maria Anna of Austria's stay in Milan as she was traveling to join her betrothed Philip IV of Spain. To celebrate the event, Bartolomeo had constructed a gallery leading into the garden, adorned with golden brocades, dancing fountains, and paintings, ending at a huge table set for a sumptuous feast. The reception was attended by the cream of the cream of society, on whom the count lavished extraordinary, priceless gifts.

Santa Maria delle Grazie

In Santa Maria delle Grazie, one of Milan's most suggestive churches, both architecture and history take on unusual tones of grandeur. It was the Dominican friars, who were building their monastery on the site, who in 1463 commissioned Guiniforte Solari to construct the majestic sacred edifice—which despite its early start was destined to be completed only in 1490. The site was already dear to the hearts of the faithful, since here rose a chapel holding a long-venerated fresco of the *Madonna delle Grazie* from which the new church was to take its name. The church was conceived in a daring Gothic-Renaissance style, with a sober gabled facade of Lombard matrix, punctuated with one-light windows and oculi. The completed and consecrated church much pleased even Ludovico il Moro, who decided to make of it a solemn funerary monument for himself and for his wife Beatrice d'Este. And to this end, in 1492 he charged Donato Bramante with demolishing the presbytery and apse and replacing them with an stunning *tribune*, in Renaissance style, surmounted by a polygonal tambour with an elegant cupola and embellished with splendid decorations (ornamental strips with the Sforza coats-of-arms and medallions with *portraits of Saints*). Beatrice d'Este was buried in this church in 1497, but due to politi-

cal adversities the same resting-place was denied Ludovico: thus the statues sculpted by Solari for the Sforza dukes' funeral monument were transferred to the Certosa of Pavia, where they still stand. From 1558 to 1782 Santa Maria delle Grazie was the seat of the Court of the Inquisition. The church was entirely restored in 1934-1937 by the architect Piero Portaluppi and again in 1947 after it had been severely damaged in the 1943 bombings. The **interior** is divided into a nave and two aisles paced by ogival arches, with *frescoes* attributable to the brushes of true masters of the Lombard Renaissance (Bernardino Butinone, Bernardino Zenale, and Gaudenzio Ferrari) and square-plan *chapels* along the aisles. Another interesting feature is the 15th-16th century *choir*, with its two orders of beautifully inlaid stalls, that graces the presbytery. At the end of the left aisle we instead find the *Chapel of the Madonna delle Grazie*, which incorporated the earlier sacellum, first enlarging it and later setting the whole in a cornice of stuccowork and frescoes. On the altar, a panel created in the 15th century for Count Gaspare da Vimercate, the owner of the land on which the church and chapel were built, depicts the Madonna delle Grazie, an image that was elicited especially fervent veneration during the plague epidemics of 1576 and 1630. The tribune gives access to the elegant, squared-off and porticoed *small cloister* built by Donato Bramante for Ludovico il Moro. And from

Below, the characteristic profile of Santa Maria delle Grazie and, left, an aerial view in which the structure of the complex, and in particular of the cloisters, is clearly visible. Next page, a suggestive image of the superbly elegant interior of Bramante's dome.

The History of a Restoration Effort

he origin of the extreme fragility shown by
Leonardo's masterpiece, besides the humidity
attributable to the natural characteristics of the
wall itself, was the experimental technique used by
the ingenious Tuscan master on this occasion:
instead of painting "a fresco" he used tempera over
a plaster base. What Vasari termed in 1568 a near-
total disaster inspired many to attempt to repaint
and/or consolidate the work—and in many cases,
these attempts at a cure were worse than the ill-
ness. Even Cardinal Federico Borromeo lent his
hand to the effort, calling in experts and techni-
cians. All with scarce results, however, especially if
it is true that halfway through the 17th century the

Dominicans (having, apparently, given up the
restoration battle as a lost cause) decided to widen
the door that opened below the work at the feet of
the figure of Christ, and had no qualms about cut-
ting off the legs of the Redeemer and two disciples.
In 1726, Michelangelo Bellotti completely repaint-
ed Leonardo's masterpiece, in oils; in 1776,
Giuseppe Mazza cleaned it; twenty-six years later,
Napoleon tried—in vain—to destine the refectory
for non-military uses, and a short time later, in fact,
the room became a stabling facility. In 1855,
Stefano Barezzi tackled restoration, and was followed in 1908 by Cavenaghi and in 1924 by
Silvestri. All this to-do certainly slowed the deterio-

ration of the work, but it was not sufficient to keep Gabriele D'Annunzio from expressing his horror at its state, apparent at first sight, in his *Ode per la morte di un capolavoro* ("Ode on the Death of a Masterpiece") composed on 6 January 1901. Spared from the 1943 bombings together with Donato Montorfano's *Crucifixion* (1495) that hung on the facing wall (while the rest of the refectory fell into pitiful ruin), the *Last Supper* was once again cleaned in 1953 by Mauro Pelliccioli, who with infinite patience attempted to eliminate the remains of the repainting efforts that had gone

before. After it had been more or less restored in conformity with Leonardo's original intentions, the Artistic and Historical Assets Office of the City of Milan subjected it to another, complex restoration action conducted by Pinin Brambilla Barcilon, which lasted from the 1970's until 1999. This action brought entire parts of Leonardo's original work back to their original splendor and has offered us the possibility, fragmentary though it may be, to once again, for the first time after many centuries, enjoy both the artist's masterful artistry and the extraordinary beauty of the work itself.

here, we can enter another of Bramante's excellent creations: the *old sacristy*.

The church is still flanked by there still stands the complex that was once the Dominican monastery, with its three cloisters (including the one by Bramante just mentioned); today, it is known above all for the large rectangular **refectory** in which Leonardo da Vinci had occasion to work (Cenacolo Vinciano).

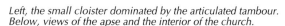

Left, the small cloister dominated by the articulated tambour. Below, views of the apse and the interior of the church.

San Maurizio al Monastero Maggiore

Built between 1503 and 1518 inside the Monastero Maggiore, the convent of the Benedictine nuns, perhaps by Gian Giacomo Dolcebuono, the church of San Maurizio was immediately divided into two sectors. The first, on Corso Magenta, was open to the faithful; the second was the nuns' choir and was separated from the first by a partition across the nave. In correspondence to the altar there was a hole, the so-called *comunichino* through which the nuns received Communion. Why all these precautions? Because the nuns were prohibited from accessing the area open to the public and communicating with the people, a prohibition that remained in force until 1794. The recently-restored church is notable for the splendor of its 16th-century frescoes that in practice cover all the surfaces of the single nave, the presbytery, the chapels, the vaults, and even the dividing wall. Here we can admire the work of many artists, including Paolo Lomazzo and Bernardino Luini (one of the maximum exponents of 16th-century Lombard art, who certainly frescoed the partition and the *Besozzi Chapel*, where we can see the master's last work, *Scenes of the Life and Martyrdom of Saint Catherine of Alexandria*, painted in 1530); and then there are works by Luini's two sons and by Vincenzo Foppa, to name just a few. The result is a composite decorative scheme in perfect harmony with the splendidly elegant Renaissance architecture of the church. Even the *women's galleries* are fully decorated, probably by Giovanni Antonio Boltraffio (1510).

Adjacent to the church, with its plain three-story *facade* punctuated by pilaster strips, is the ancient *cloister*, an artifact from the original convent (destroyed in 1799 by the revolutionary upheavals). In the garden we find two *towers*, also from the Roman era: one quadrangular and the other polygonal, later incorporated into Emperor Maximianus' walls.

The Circus

The church of San Maurizio rises on the ancient site of the Roman Circus Maximus, built by Emperor Maximianus, that extended from Porta Ticinese to Porta Magenta.

With its 505 meters' length and 80 meters' width, it was one of the largest circuses of Roman times and was still in use under Lombardic rule. The outlines of the circus are still discernable in the urban fabric of modern Milan, in the area delimited by Via Brisa, Via del Torchio, and Via Luini.

The church of San Maurizio al Monastero Maggiore is home to splendid frescoes: right, the dividing wall with works by Bernardino Luini; top right, The Martyrdom of Saint Maurizio; left, Vincenzo Foppa's Saint Matthew.

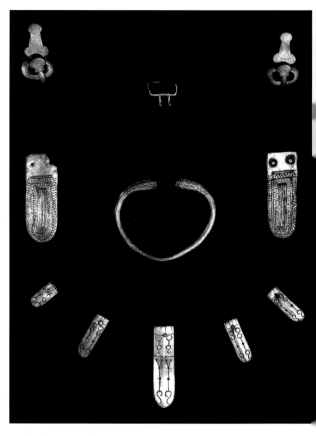

Top, the courtyard of the Civico Museo Archeologico, with the polygonal tower and the remains of the Roman walls and right, a composition of objects of Longobard manufacture, with a bracelet and various belt fittings. Bottom left, an elaborate Gothic buckle and, right, a splendid silver plate decorated with the figure of a fisherman.

Civico Museo Archeologico

The cloister of the ancient Monastero Maggiore in Corso Magenta today holds and exhibits the well-stocked Etruscan, Greek, and Roman collections of the Civico Museo Archeologico di Milano, founded in 1965 and since then in continual and constant expansion. These collections are of great importance since they offer an extraordinary wealth of documentation about these ancient, sophisticated civilizations. Tomb furnishings, works in *bucchero*, bronze objects and statues, urns, and canopic jars illustrate the culture of Etruria; ceramics and vases in various styles and types of decoration tell us about Greece; and statues, portraits, large mosaics, cups, and items in silver celebrate the greatness and magnificence of the civilization of ancient Rome. There is also a prestigious epigraphic collection. Very interesting the section exhibiting the archaeological finds donated by the State of Israel to the promoters of the so-called "Caesarea Archeological Mission," which from 1959 to 1964 conducted the rediscovery, in this Israeli locality, of the great Roman theater and the mighty circle of walls that surrounded the ancient city of Herod. The prehistoric material is instead now housed in the majestic rooms of the Castello Sforzesco.

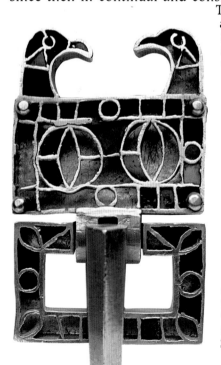

Piazza degli Affari

Construction of Piazza Affari, in the center of the Milan neighborhood destined to take its name, began in 1926. Today it is the fulcrum of financial Milan, of negotiations, of stock trading, and of important investments. And here, not far from the church of San Maurizio, we only naturally find the grandiose, snow-white **Palazzo della Borsa Valori** (Stock Exchange building) designed and built in 1931 by Paolo Mezzanotte. Four colossal columns, adorned at their bases and tops by sculptural groups (in particular, the *Four Elements* by Leone Lodi and Geminiano Cibau), mark the travertine facade. In the interior, a glass vault lights the vast *Salone della Borsa Valori*, on three floors. In a curious mix of past and present, the lower levels of this building, where the bustling life of present-day financial Milan converges and flares, we note the remains of the ancient Roman theater built in the 1st century AD and demolished in the 12th century by Frederick Barbarossa. It was a quite respectable structure, with a spectator capacity of about 7000.

Tempio della Vittoria

Dedicated to the fallen of World War I (about 10,000, whose names are inscribed on bronze plates preserved in the *crypt*), the Tempio della Vittoria (Temple of Victory) was built between 1927 and 1930 by Giovanni Muzio. It was damaged during the 1943 bombings and later restored. Resembling a tall, octagonal tower, the marble monument rises within an elegant enclosure; at its summit, a bronze *lantern* housing a *beacon*, the light from which is visible from many miles away.

Right, the Salone della Borsa; bottom, the facade of the Palazzo della Borsa.

Basilica di Sant'Ambrogio

One of the oldest churches in Milan and one of the most interesting of all medieval religious buildings, construction of the basilica of Sant'Ambrogio began, on the site of the Christian cemetery (*Ad Martyres*) outside of Porta Vercellina, in 379 AD. The church was small in size, with a nave and two aisles, with no transept and with a barely roughed-out apse. Seven years later, on 13 January, it was consecrated by Bishop Saint Ambrose, who died in

Images of the grandiose Basilica di Sant'Ambrogio: the exterior of the church, the facade seen from the wide portico standing before it, and an aerial view of the entire complex. On the facing page, the solemn, luminous interior.

and by the 10th century the ancient basilica proved totally inadequate—above all in terms of size—to meet the changed needs of the city, civic and religious. And thus began the prolonged and demanding work of enlarging and restructuring the basilica. The work invested above all the atrium (a pre-existing structure built in the 9th century by order of Milan's then-archbishop Anspert), the nave and aisles, and the presbytery. The endeavor culminated in construction of the new apse, the new, higher tambour, and in 1128-1144, the left bell tower in Lombard Romanesque style, now known as the *Campanile dei Canonici*. It was, however, really completed only in 1889 with construction of the minor loggia. In the 1400's, even Donato Bramante contributed to beautifying the great complex. On commission from Cardinal Ascanio Sforza, he built the cloisters and the *Portico della Canonica*. Begun in 1492, work was suspended seven years later when Ludovico il Moro fell from power (only the side adjacent to the basilica was completed; it was damaged in the World War II bombings, restored, and in 1955 given a second side, in perfect Bramantesque style, by Ferdinando Reggiori).

Many and diverse were the actions that followed in the centuries after Bramante; in fact, so diversified were they that in 1857 Archduke Maximilian of Hapsburg felt the need to restore the original, plain

Top, a view of the light-filled nave of Sant'Ambrogio; below, a detail of the pulpit

A suggestive image of the San Vittore chapel.

odor of sanctity and was in fact later to become Milan's beloved patron saint. Ambrose was buried here in 397 AD in the crypt as we see it today, alongside the mortal remains of Saints Gervasius and Protasius, to whom the original *Basilica Martyrum* had been dedicated until that time.

In the late 8th century, with the approbation of the archbishop Pietro, the Benedictines built their convent adjacent to the basilica—thus inaugurating a period of not always convivial cohabitation with the clergy, which, what is more, was sanctioned in 789 by a Carolingian decree. Between 822 and 859 the basilica also acquired the sober, linear bell tower that stands to its right and is now better known as the *Campanile dei Monaci*. The city grew,

Saint Ambrose

Ambrose was born in Trier in Gaul, where his father was prefect, in 334 or 339. After completing his studies in Rome, he was sent to Milan as governor of Liguria and Emilia. At the death of the Arian bishop Auxentius in 374, Ambrose was acclaimed new bishop of the city by the populace, who appreciated his humanity and his courage; only afterwards was he baptized and took the Holy Orders. He was a Doctor of the Church, generous and untiring in his defense of the faith

and in the conversion of pagans, atheists, heretics, and Arians (the conversion of Saint Augustine was his work), a pastor deeply loved by his people. At his death on 4 April 397, Ambrose immediately became the patron saint of Milan. He is celebrated on 7 December, the day of his ordination as bishop.

lines of the basilica by eliminating the disfigurements that had gone before, with particular regard for the decorations and the Neoclassical and Baroque additions. The complex was seriously damaged in 1943, but under the supervision of the architect Ferdinando Reggiori it was rapidly restored and returned to conditions fitting its status. The basilica stands below the current level of the square and seems almost to hide behind the elegant 12th-century *atrium* with its rectangular portico, the pillars of which end in splendid *capitals* sculpted with phytomorphic, zoomorphic, and anthropomorphic figures, largely redone in the 1600's by Richini. On the walls under the porticoes are series of bas-reliefs, pagan and early Christian inscriptions, memorial stones, and even the *sarcophagus of Archbishop Anspert*, who died in 881. The rear porticoed side, which constitutes the narthex of the facade, is surmounted by another loggia with five degrading arches delineating a gabled facade typical of the Lombard style. Three *portals* open on the facade; the two at the sides are embellished with mighty architraves and marvelous decorations taken from the medieval bestiaries. The center portal is closed by two bronze wings from the 11th-12th century. Its

original wooden doors, with panels of *Scenes from the Lives of David and Saul* (4th-7th century) are today preserved (unfortunately in a fragmentary state) in the Basilica's museum, while what we now see on the portal are 18th-century copies. In the interior, composite pillars separate the nave and aisles; they were erected in the early 11th century to replace the earlier columns. On high, above the aisles, large archways mark out the women's galleries that face on the nave, which is illuminated by three wide windows opened in the facade to compensate for the progressive decrease in natural light as larger and larger buildings were constructed around the basilica. At the end of the right aisle, a railing gives access to the **Sacellum of San Vittore in Ciel d'Oro**, built in the 4th century over the ancient *Cimitero ad Martyres* to guard the remains of Saint Victor and later those of Ambrose's brother, Saint Satyrus. Frequently restored, it is a square hall surmounted by a small dome, gleaming with ancient mosaics. The precious and quite elaborate sculptural decoration is clearly stratified in different stylistic periods. From the 9th century, the grandiose **gold altar**, an extraordinary product of Lombard goldsmithery designed and partially realized by Volvinio, with *Scenes from the Lives of Christ and Saint Ambrose* graven on gold sheets on the front part and on gilded silver on the back; and the *baldachin* above the altar, on four porphyry columns probably from the original 4th-century version. The *pulpit*, over an *early-Christian sarcophagus of man and wife* (4th century), was almost certainly rebuilt in the 13th century from pieces of the original pulpit, splintered in the 1196 collapse of the bay in front of the tambour. Interesting the reliefs with *Scenes from the Old and New Testament*. The luminous *mosaic* that decorates the conch of the apse is in part composed of the mosaic of *The Preaching of Saint Ambrose* that once must have dominated the original apse (before the church was enlarged in the 9th century). From the 9th century also are the figures of *Saints Gervasius and Protasius*; from the 11th the *Christ Enthroned*; from the 12th, the medallions at his feet

The striking monument to Saint Francis in the Basilica di Sant'Ambrogio.

Museo della Basilica di Sant'Ambrogio

The Museo della Basilica di Sant'Ambrogio (Museum of the Basilica of Saint Ambrose) was founded in 1949 to protect and valorize the precious treasure of the ancient church and the innumerable curios that testify to its long and complex history. Access to the museum is through the Portico of the Canonica. Visitors are immediately struck by the beautiful goldwork: notable, a 15th-century *processional cross*. Next is the *Sala degli Arazzi* (Hall of Tapestries) with marvelous creations by the Flemish school; then the *Sala delle Stoffe* or Hall of Fabrics, with the famous *dalmatic of Saint Ambrose*, (perhaps the shroud that wrapped the saint's body) and fabrics from his sarcophagus and other early Christian sepulchers. Following is the *Sala dei Paliotti* (Hall of the Altarpieces), where we can admire the triptych of the *Virgin and Saints Ambrose and Jerome* by Bernardino Zenale (1494), and the *Sala della Lettiera*, so-called after the bedstead on display here, on which Saint Ambrose is said to have died. This room also contains the reconstruction of the original wooden doors of the central portal of the basilica, with significative fragments and original wooden panels from the 4th century. Going on, we come to the *Sala degli Affreschi* (Hall of Frescoes), with works by Bergognone, Zenale, and Luini

Left, the baldachin at the center of the presbytery
Below, one side of the sarcophagus called "of Stilicho," under the pulpit.

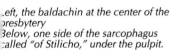

as well as manuscripts on parchment illustrating the evolution of the miniature from the 10th through the 18th century, and to the *Sala delle Vicende Storiche*, where 17th-century tapestries, documents, prints, and drawings review the history of the basilica. Also interesting—and somewhat disquieting, are the shells of the bombs that in 1943 fell on the basilica, devastating it, and today are on exhibit as a reminder and a warning. The *Archivio Capitolare* (Chapter Archives), preserved in the museum, count a well-stocked library, more than 1500 parchments, and scores of manuscripts, but the showpiece is undoubtedly *Gian Galeazzo Visconti's Missal*, splendidly illuminated in 1395 by Anovelo da Imbonate.

Top, a detail of the gold altar created by Volvinio in the 9th century.
Above, Roman sarcophagi found during restoration work in the basilica and arranged in the portico in front of the entrance.

Museo Nazionale della Scienza e della Tecnica Leonardo da Vinci

Created in 1947 and dedicated to the man who, with his extraordinary intuitions and genial inventions was a precursor of modern science and technology, this museum, with its 28 sections that trace a thorough panorama of the most disparate sectors of science and technology and its 15,000 items on about 40,000 square meters exhibit space, is in part located in a monumental building in the former *Monastero degli Olivetani*, where we also find the splendid 16th-century *cloisters*. This is the section dedicated to analysis and models of *Leonardo's extraordinary machines*—but also to astronomy, graphic arts and goldworking, metallurgy, computer science (of note the well-equipped Internet Laboratory), clock-making, motorcycles, automobiles, and musical instruments. Everything here is presented with the aid of interactive laboratories that permit the visitor to directly experiment with inventions, technologies, and theories. Then there is the picturesque *Padiglione Ferroviario*, a real railway station in Liberty style that houses twenty or so locomotives and railway cars, and a number of characteristic trams. The exhibits in the phantasmagoric *Edificio Aeronavale* target analysis of the rela-

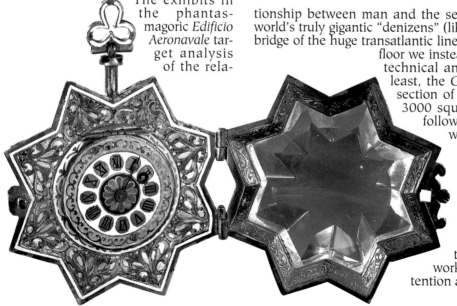

Sala dell'Orologeria: above, a reconstruction by Luigi Pippa of Giovanni de' Dondi's famous astrarium; below, a rock-crystal pocket watch by Jacot des Combe (Vienna, late 17th century), with silver case and enameled face.

tionship between man and the sea and include some of the water world's truly gigantic "denizens" (like the *Ebe* sailing ship and the pilot bridge of the huge transatlantic liner *Conte Biancamano*). On the upper floor we instead find numerous airplanes of great technical and historical interest. Last but not least, the *Giardini della Scienza*, the open-air section of the museum: on an area of about 3000 square meters, where the visitor can follow scientific "trails" and experiment with interactive machines. The museum's exhibits are continually updated and added to, and represent an authentic point of reference for the cultural and scientific life of Milan—and not Milan alone. But we must not forget that the ancient convent that houses a part of the collections, with its interesting structures, is in itself a work of art quite equally worthy of attention and admiration.

Pinacoteca Ambrosiana

The Pinacoteca Ambrosiana was born of the love for art and beauty that distinguished its creator, Cardinal Federico Borromeo, who in 1618 decided it would be a worthy complement to the pre-existing *Biblioteca Ambrosiana* (today the repository of an inestimable treasure in manuscripts, miniatures, and drawings, including Leonardo da Vinci's famous *Codex Atlanticus*). Two years later, he also founded the *Accademia del Disegno* (transferred in 1775 to Brera by order of the Austrian government, with the name of Accademia di Belle Arti). Part of a far-reaching and surprisingly modern cultural project, the Pinacoteca originally housed "only" the collection of paintings, sculptures, and prints donated by Borromeo, who also commissioned the building that was to be its home: the *Palazzo dell'Ambrogiano* designed by the architect Fabio Mangone and completed in 1630. The picture gallery encompassed 172 works, a good half of which on religious subjects (just think, for example, of Titian's *Adoration of the Magi* and the works by Bernardino Luini, Bor-

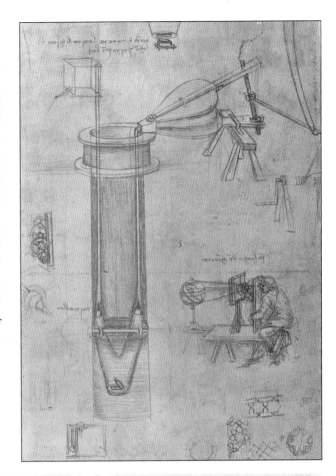

A machine for raising water, from a sheet of Leonardo da Vinci's *Codex Atlanticus, in the Biblioteca Ambrosiana.*

Portrait of Saint Charles Borromeo.

Federico Borromeo

Federico Borromeo, cousin of Saint Charles
and a figure of outstanding human
and spiritual qualities, but also cultured
and sensitive to the fascination of the arts,
was born in 1564 to one of the
most important and wealthiest families
of the Lombardy of the times.
Ordained cardinal at just 23 years of age
by Pope Sixtus V, who called him to Rome,
Federico became Archbishop of Milan in 1595.
From that time on all his energies were dedicated
to the diocese and its souls.
And this is the also the key to understanding
Federico's great love for art:
an patron of the arts and a friend of artists,
a connoisseur of religious painting
and the naturalistic Flemish school alike,
he was always a profound believer
in the strong didactic and doctrinal influence that
art could exert on the faithful.

romeo's favorite artist). To the original collection the art-patron cardinal continued to add the creations of some of the most prestigious artists, and often true masterworks like Caravaggio's *Fruit Basket*, purchased by Borromeo in 1626, and the cartoon of Raphael's *School of Athens*. Over the centuries, this prestigious institution changed and expanded, with new, significative acquisitions (like the *Madonna del Padiglione* ["Madonna of the Pavilion"] by Sandro Botticelli and the *de Petris donation*, which consisted of a precious collection of gilded bronzes), to the point that it also provided a representative survey of

the artistic manifestations of the 1800's. Inevitably, this progressive development made demanded reconsideration and adaptation of the exhibit spaces, which were considerably enlarged between 1929 and 1931. More recently, in 1997, following six entire years of painstaking restoration, the Pinacoteca (still an institution very much at the forefront) greeted the public with a new arrangement: 24 rooms in which the works are exhibited in chronological order and are accompanied by detailed information regarding their origin in such a manner as to clearly identify the original Borromeo nucleus.

Leonardo da Vinci, *Portrait of a Musician*

Painted in 1484-1485, this oil on canvas is one of the few male portraits by Leonardo—and in any case it is the only one remaining to us. It portrays a musician, perhaps that Franchino Gaffurio who was the first great master of the *Cappella Musicale*. Of a noble family, the musician studied Latin literature and music; after having taken the Holy Orders, he became Master of the Choir of the Duomo of Milan on 22 January 1484 and held the post until his death. Leonardo's portrait is characterized by marked psychological introspection: the subject is portrayed holding a sheet of music on which appear the letters "Cant ... Ang...". We might complete the inscription as "*Cantum Angelicum ac Divinum Opus*," the title of one of Gaffurio's works. The man appears in a state of intense concentration, gazing into the distance, a moment before he begins his hymn.

Ambrogio de Predis, *Portrait of a Lady*

When this painting was acquired by the Pinacoteca Ambrosiana in 1618, it was defined as "*Ritratto d'una Duchessa dal mezzo in su, di mano di Leonardo*" ("Portrait of a Duchess from the waist up, by Leonardo's hand"). This attribution remained for a long time, above all since the painting was matched with the *Portrait of a Musician* in the hypothesis that the two figures may have represented Ludovico il Moro and Beatrice d'Este.
Once this identification had been proved false, the critics came up with many others as to whom the beautiful woman might be: Bianca Maria Sforza, Isabella of Castile and Aragon, an illegitimate daughter of the Duke of Milan, and many others. *Rorida fanciulla di pastosa bellezza* ("dewy-cheeked girl of mellow beauty") as she was defined by Franco Russoli, is perhaps still the best appellation ever for this painting, in which Ambrogio de Predis, a faithful disciple of Leonardo, so admirably succeeds in blending preciously lustrous color and an unwavering light.

Bernardino Luini, *Nursing Madonna.*

Recently restored and probably dating to the 1620's, this refined panel in oils and tempera, with its elegant and finely-drawn lines, matches references to Leonardo da Vinci and equally obvious reminiscences of Raphael, in the drapery as in the profiles and the shadings of color.

Caravaggio, *Fruit Basket (La Fiscella)*

Everything (or almost everything) that could be written about this still life has been. It is almost a repeat performance of the fruit basket on the table in the foreground of the *The Supper at Emmaus* (London)—so much so as to lead us to think that Caravaggio first painted the *Supper* and then reproduced the precious detail in a separate painting. Federico Borromeo, who had acquired the painting in Rome from Cardinal Del Monte in 1596 and who wanted a *pendant*, expressed himself thus: "I would have liked to set alongside it another, similar basket, but since no one could ever have again achieved the incomparable beauty and excellence of this one, it had to remain alone." In its simplicity and essentiality, this is an absolutely perfect still life: from below, the beautifully represented basket (the *fiscella*) exalts the fruits and the leaves, which stand out against the light-colored wall. Caravaggio asserted that he painted figures and flowers with the same degree of commitment, and that for him there did not exist any difference between these two painting genres. Thus, it is precisely the absence of the human element that so heightens the realism of the object represented, of which we see the smallest details, painted as they are with cold objectivity. The luster, the transparency, the textures of the various types of fruit in the painting make this one of the great archetypes of Italian painting.

Palazzo di Brera

The impressive Palazzo di Brera rises on the site where in the 14th century there stood an austere monastery of the Fratres Humiliati. In 1572, the Jesuits took their place and established their school here. In the early 17th century the architect Francesco Maria Richini, commissioned by the religious order, dedicated all his mastery and energies to building a truly splendid edifice. In truth, the realization went well beyond the life span of the designer, who died in 1658 leaving the work in the hands of his son Gian Domenico; it then passed to Girolamo Quadrio, and was finally completed by Pietro Giorgio Rossone. The building could be said to have been completed only in 1773; but as soon afterward as 1780 Piermarini intervened to add another touch of sober elegance with the addition of the majestic portal. Today, this austere building, a typical example of Lombard Baroque architecture, surrounding the marvelous rectangular courtyard with its two orders of arcades on coupled columns, hosts important cultural institutions, from the *Osservatorio Astronomico* to the *Orto Botanico* and from the *Istituto Lombardo di Scienze e Lettere* to the *Biblioteca* and the *Accademia di Belle Arti*. What is more, the entire complex was deliberately consecrated to public celebration of the illustrious figures whose names were in one or another manner linked to that of the institution in Brera. Thus, alongside the bronze *statue* of Napoleon in the guise of Mars the Peacemaker, cast in 1809 in Rome to a model by Canova, there appeared monuments to patrons of the arts, benefactors, artists, and scientists. To name just a few of the most prestigious: the *monument to Cesare Beccaria* by Pompeo Marchesi and that to *Giuseppe Parini* by Gaetano Monti, which watch over the monumental staircase. But, above all, this noble palazzo is home to one of the most precious jewels in Milan's entire cultural and artistic panorama: the **Pinacoteca di Brera**.

A view of the grand courtyard of the Palazzo di Brera and, right, a detail of the statue of Napoleon, a masterpiece in bronze by Canova.

Pinacoteca di Brera

The original nucleus of the collections in the Pinacoteca di Brera sprang from the accumulation of paintings, in the Palazzo di Brera, requisitioned from churches and convents suppressed during the Napoleonic era (1798). Quite soon, however, the gallery affirmed its vocation for teaching, flanking the Accademia di Belle Arti founded by order of Maria Theresa of Austria in 1776. It was thanks to the commitment and the impassioned work of a secretary of the academy, Giuseppe Bossi, that beginning in the early 19th century the gallery's holdings increased to the point that in just a few years it was possible to open four rooms on the first floor containing a series of portraits and self-portraits of painters and a number of the masterpieces destined to become true symbols of this prestigious Milanese institution, like the *Marriage of the Virgin* by Raphael (1504), Gentile Bellini's *Madonna and Child* (1510), and Bramantino's *Crucifixion*, from the early 16th century. During the Napoleonic era, Brera enjoyed special consideration, if it is true that in that period the Pinacoteca was enriched by innumerable very important works selected, purchased, or requisitioned by the museum curator Andrea Appiani in the most disparate areas of the Kingdom of Italy, of which Milan was then the capital. Thus, to Brera came true masterpieces from the Veneto region, and others, in 1811, from Bologna, including paintings by the Carracci's, Guido Reni, Francesco Albani, and Guercino. In 1813, an agreement stipulated with Paris' Louvre gave the Milanese Pinacoteca a prestigious and representative selection of the 17th-century Flemish school, with five paintings by Rubens, Jordaens, Van Dyck, and Rembrandt.

And in the meantime, while the spectacular Napoleonic Rooms, still the heart of the Brera complex, were taking shape, the church acquired an authentic treasure of detached frescoes by Bernardino Luini, Gaudenzio Ferrari, Vincenzo Foppa, Bergognone, and Bramantino. Other paintings were instead subtracted from the Archbishop of Milan's picture gallery, property of the city Curia. In the decades following the fall of Napoleon, development and expansion of the Pinacoteca of Brera con-

A image revealing all the vastness and sheer splendor of the elegant Napoleonic Rooms in the Pinacoteca di Brera.

Bramantino, *Holy Family*

Bramantino (Bartolomeo Suardi) painted this *Holy Family* in which the male figure is a portrayal of Gian Giacomo Trivulzio, in 1512. The painting is notable for the intellectual content, which permeates and infringes on the devotional sentiments. But despite this fact, the work was purchased in 1650 by a godly man, the cardinal Cesare Monti, who fully appreciated its extraordinary artistic qualities.

Vincenzo Foppa,
Saint Sebastian

Dated about 1485 and originally on a wall of the sacristy of the church of Santa Maria di Brera, his fresco, which was detached in 1808, demonstrates how profound was Foppa's knowledge of perspective and its problems, probably acquired through analysis of the works of Donatello, Paolo Uccello, Andrea del Castagno, and Mantegna. The mastery of Foppa's painting demonstrates that he had little to learn from Bramante, who at the time had been in Milan for some years.

Correggio, *The Adoration of the Magi*

A work of extraordinary dramatic vigor, this canvas reveals how well Correggio had assimilated important lessons in art "imparted" by Leonardo, Raphael, and Giorgione, to name just a few of the masters closest in time. But it is also a clear expression of how far the artist, with his irrepressible, explosive creative flair, had gone beyond the influence of Mantegna.

Tiziano, *Cenacolo*

Probably a sketch for the grandiose *Last Supper* that Titian painted in 1557-1564 for the Spanish king Philip II and which was later moved to the Escurial. This large canvas is extremely important for understanding how the other painting was originally conceived (but later deprived of the upper portion), but is also important due to its significative links to Leonardo da Vinci's *Last Supper*, which Titian saw during a stay in Milan in the mid 1500's.

Vittore Carpaccio, *Presentation in the Temple*

In 1504, Vittore Carpaccio was called in to decorate the Albanese School then being built near San Maurizio with a cycle of six episodes from the life of the Virgin. Scattered among various museums after being requisitioned in 1811, all the works in the cycle (including this *Presentation in the Temple*), although perhaps actually painted by the master's assistants, unequivocally denote Carpaccio's hand both as regards composition and in the extreme attention to particulars, the wealth of details, and the exquisite definition both of the subject and of its representation.

Giovanni e Gentile Bellini, *Saint Mark Preaching in Alexandria*

Painted for the Confraternity of Saint Mark, this majestic canvas (3.47 x 7.70 m) was left unfinished by Gentile Bellini at his death in 1507 and was completed by his brother Giovanni. Against a background of spectacular, well-articulated architecture, the group of opulently-dressed spectators probably includes portraits of figures who were well-known and easily recognizable at the time.

Pompeo Batoni, *Holy Family with Saints Zachary and Elizabeth, and the Infant John*

A felicitous and skilful selection of carefully-studied palette colors and a likewise pondered compositive balance make this painting a splendid synthesis of the international Rococo culture and 17th-century Bolognese classicism, winning its author well-earned place among the pioneers of Italian Neoclassicism.

Guercino, *Abraham Casting Out Hagar and Ishmael*

Giovanni Francesco Barbieri, better known as Guercino, succeeded in permeating this rather late work (dated to 1657-1658) with such a refined and erudite Neoclassical atmosphere and stylistic definition that it became a model for all the Neoclassical and academic painting of the 18th and 19th centuries.

Andrea Mantegna, *Madonna and Child with Angels*

Styled for the church of Santa Maria Maggiore, in Venice, in about 1485, this expressive *Madonna* incorporates profound reminiscences of Venetian painting in general and the painting of Giovanni Bellini in particular, even though Mantegna had been living and working in Mantua for many years when he painted it.

Lorenzo Lotto, *Pietà*

This dramatic work by Lotto was painted in 1545; that is, at the close of the artist's last stay in Treviso. It unites, with its dramatic pyramid of figures, the la medieval theme of the Virgin holding the dead Chris on her knees and the overwhelming sense of involvement and emotional transport typical of Mannerism.

Piero della Francesca, *Virgin and Saints w
Federico da Montefel*

A painting of truly extraordinary brightness a
luminosity, a work of true perfectionism framed in t
niche of an elaborate, deep, and carefully-studi
perspective, this *Virgin with Saints* is one of 1
master's later works. Accurate restoration h
revealed it to be probably unfinishe

Raffaello,
Marriage of the Virgin

A panel planed with great care according to precise criteria of monumental architecture, the *Marriage of the Virgin* (1504) hinges on a center axis delineated by the figure of the priest and the looming entrance of the great and perfected Temple. The whole gives an impression of perfect balance and harmonious solemnity.

Maestro di Santa Colomba, *Scenes from the Life of Saint Colomba*

Composed of three panels, with a precise narrative line and a clean-cut volumetric arrangement, this 14th-century masterpiece is one of the most elegant and perfect works of the post-Giotto schools.

Caravaggio, *Supper at Emmaus*

With its dark, mellow colors and figures of clearly popular matrix, this canvas, painted in 1606, fits well in that gallery of works by Caravaggio that shift sacred events toward the plane of everyday life and the common people. And this was a choice that cost the artist to be shunned by the more traditionally-minded and dogmatic ecclesiastical hierarchies.

Donato Bramante, *Christ at the Column*

Painted for the Abbazia di Chiaravalle, this extraordinarily expressive *Christ* marked a true turning point in the lives of that circle of artists working in Ludovico il Moro's late 15th century Milan. The work was acquired by the Pinacoteca di Brera in 1915; a major concern in the move was to guarantee better conditions for its conservation.

Silvestro Lega, *The Pergola*

Signed and dated 1868, this canvas with its sedate, refined, and intriguing elegance is without doubt one of the finest creations of the Tuscan "Macchiaioli" painters, uniting as it does reminiscences of a noble artistic past (Beato Angelico, Piero della Francesca) and sensitivity to the interesting formal novelties that were gaining ground in that period, especially in France.

tinued, perhaps more slowly than before but constantly and without interruption. The by-then vast museum, enriched by bequests, donations, and purchases (that brought in works of the caliber of Mantegna's famous *Dead Christ*, purchased by the heirs to Giuseppe Bossi's post in 1824, and the *Madonna of the Rosary* by Luini, in 1826), finally became independent of the Accademia di Belle Arti in 1882. To the Accademia nevertheless remained a goodly number of the 19th-century canvases. Rearranged by the competent hand of the extremely active director Giuseppe Bertini (1882-1898), the Pinacoteca also continued to grow through acquisition of more works of especial value: from the *Amanti Veneziani* ("*Venetian Lovers*") by Paris Bordon to Bronzino's *Portrait of Andrea Doria as Neptune* and from the *Adoration of the Magi* by Correggio to Bramantino's *Holy Family*. The latter works, once again, came from the archbishopric collections. A new arrangement by schools of painting and chronological order was in the meantime planned and over time implemented. Thus, with the

Amedeo Modigliani,
Woman's Head

This *Woman's Head*, painted in 1915, is a work of great interest above all for the schematic simplifications which Modigliani almost certainly derived from knowledge of the art of Black Africa and which very effectively lend clean definition to the features (psychological and well as physical) of the subject.

new and often very important acquisitions of the first half of the 20th century (the predella of Gentile da Fabriano's *Polyptych*, the *Men-at-Arms* cycle by Bramante, yet more works by Correggio, Pietro Longhi, Tiepolo, Canaletto, and Fattori, Caravaggio's *The Supper at Emmaus*, and *The Pergola* by Silvestro Lega, to name just a few), a totally renewed Pinacoteca di Brera was inaugurated in the 1950's following restructuring work by Pietro Portaluppi and Franco Albini. It was by then a modern cultural institution, at the forefront as regards both conception and exhibits as well as for its excellent

Umberto Boccioni,
Doppio autoritratto (Self-Portrait)

Painted front and back (hence the Italian title), this was the first 20th-century work to become part of the Pinacoteca di Brera collection. It is composed of a self-portrait as a young man and another of a much older artist. It dates to 1908 and is clearly a presage of the artist's soon-to-be-manifested turn to the Futurist school.

Pablo Picasso,
Study for *Les
demoiselles d'Avignon*

This 1907 study
stands out for the
stylistic
characteristics that
clearly link it to
Futurist models while
at the same time
establishing it as an
interesting pioneering
effort in Cubism.

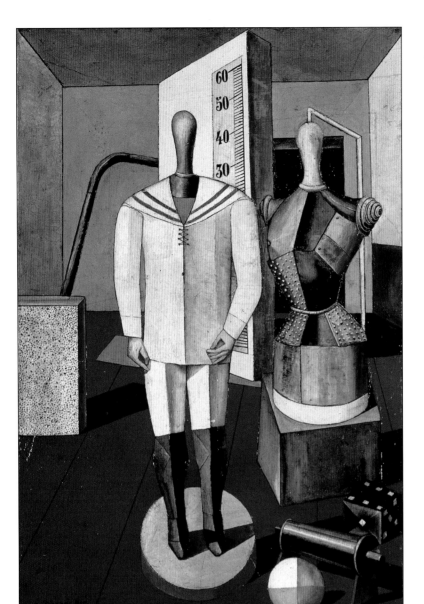

Carlo Carrà, *Mother and Child*

A classical creation of that metaphysical painting of which Carrà was as important an exponent as De Chirico, this canvas, dated 1917, exudes a fascinating sense of mystery made of unsettling geometric forms, intensely violent colors, and a profoundly-twisted sense of everyday reality.

use of the most up-to-date technologies. Then began definition of the ambitious "Grande Brera" project, which called for enlargement of the museum spaces with acquisition of the so-called *Appartamento dell'Astronomo*, where the Emilio and Maria Jesi donation was arranged; the works include masterpieces by the most prominent early 20th-century Italian artists, including Boccioni, Braque, Carrà, De Pisis, Marino Marini, Modigliani, and Morandi, and also, on consignment, twenty or so works by Futurist artists from the Jucker Collection (now at the Civico Museo di Arte Contemporanea di Milano). Another new arrangement, this time for the Napoleonic Rooms, was conceived in the 1980's. Today, the Pinacoteca di Brera is well-affirmed as a prestigious museum dear to the hearts of the Milanese, and has shown itself to be still open to new acquisitions: for instance, the bequest of Lambert Vitali, whose collection, come to Brera in the late 1990's, is now on display in the *Sala della Passione* awaiting permanent arrangement in the museum proper.

Filippo De Pisis,
Still Life

An early work by the artist (1924), this *Still Life*, with eggs, is marked by its refined sense of color selection and an almost rarified moderation of style that covertly recalls the metaphysical lesson of a Carrà or a De Chirico.

San Marco

Built in 1254 by Friar Lanfranco Settala of the Hermits of Saint Anthony on the site of an earlier church dedicated to Saint Mark in honor of the Venetians who aided the Milanese in rebuilding their city after it was devastated by Frederick Barbarossa, this basilica was more than once enlarged and transformed (in the 14th century, in 1690, and again in 1873, when the facade was entirely reconstructed in characteristic Lombard Gothic style). Surviving from the medieval church are the ogival vaults, the head of the transept, the presbytery, and the 13th-century bell tower. Along the right side of the basilica run a series of elegant chapels, while the left abuts with one side of the cloister of what as late as the 18th century was still a monastery of Augustinian friars. Decorated with marvelous *frescoes* (including one, by Leonardo's school but discovered only recently, of the *Virgin and Child blessing the young Saint John*), over the centuries the basilica of San Marco has become associated with quite a few illustrious figures: Martin Luther worshipped here when he was very young; the symphonist G. B. Sammartini was organist here in the 1700's; Wolfgang Amadeus Mozart stayed in the clergy house for three months in 1770; Giuseppe Parini attended Mass here; and on 22 May 1874 the basilica hosted the first performance of the *Requiem Mass* composed by Giuseppe Verdi for the death of Alessandro Manzoni.

The church of San Marco (right, a detail of the facade) houses many fine works of art. Top right, frescoes from various periods, representing a Crucifixion *and the* Founding of the Augustinian *Order. Top left, a detail of the frescoes by Genovesino in the cupola of the presbytery.*

Giardini Pubblici

Famous for their important role as Milan's first public park, the Giardini Pubblici boast a premier designer: they were built in 1783-1786 to plans by Giuseppe Piermarini, who in order to create the park united the kitchen-gardens and orchards (and flower-gardens) and gardens of a number of convents along Corso Venezia. Later (1857) enlarged by order of Emperor Franz Joseph and later yet progressively made over as a huge English-style garden (by Giuseppe Balzaretto first in 1862 with later work by Emilio Alemagna in 1881), the Giardini Pubblici now cover an area of 1? hectares, enhanced by luxuriant vegetation, and still—at least in part—reflect the original Neoclassical plan.

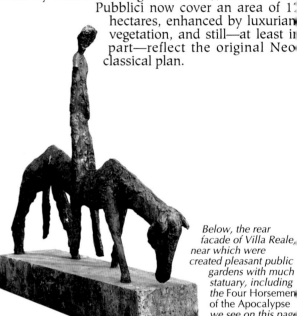

Below, the rear facade of Villa Reale, near which were created pleasant public gardens with much statuary, including the Four Horsemen of the Apocalypse we see on this page

The Tempietto dell'Amore built in the romantic Villa Reale park
and, top, the villa's ballroom.

Villa Reale

Almost as an ideal continuance of the Giardini Pubblici, opening off Via Palestro, are the pleasant romantic *gardens* with sculptures and reproductions
of ruins. Together with the Neoclassical Villa Reale
to which they look, they were created in 1790-1793
by the architect Leopold Pollack for Count Lodovi-
co Barbiano di Belgioioso. In fact, the original name
of the villa was Villa Belgioioso. The villa and
grounds were acquired in 1802 by the Cisalpine Republic and donated to Napoleon, who resided here
with his wife Josephine. Other important figures
who stayed here were the viceroy Eugène de
Beauharnais (from whom the name "Villa Reale"),
General Radetzky (who died here), and Napoleon
III. The villa has been owned by the city of Milan
since 1921. Outstanding, above all, the rear facade,
with its columns and pilasters, opening on the English-style garden. The frescoes, decorations, and
furnishings of the splendid *interiors* are in refined
Neoclassical taste, and the rooms are now home to
the **Galleria d'Arte Moderna**.

Giuseppe Pellizza da Volpedo,
The Fourth State

Pellizza da Volpedo was a complex and controversial painter who at the dawn of the 20th century had occasion to project his art in the social sphere. In the three years between 1898 and 1901 he created that which is universally considered his most important work, *The Fourth State*, a masterly fresco of a social class in vigorous evolution. The scene thus goes beyond the mere depiction of a strike or a protest: against the background of a soft sunset, harmoniously composed figures

gesture and move in manners that are anything but violent or agitated; in their sculptural boldness they form a homogeneous group that advances slowly but inexorably. The theme greatly interested Pellizza da Volpedo, who thus expressed his solidarity with the Socialist cause as part of his attempt to pluck from life images capable of representing real life while yet transforming the images on the plane of pure and essential beauty.

Giovanni Segantini, *The Two Mothers*

This painting vividly but not painfully reveals Giovanni Segantini's origins in poverty; it may have been painted in the Brianza area in 1889. Segantini, a sensitive exponent of the Divisionist movement in art, was inspired by that realism typical of pre-Impressionist French painting, identified by the artist in Millet's works.
The scene is set in an interior, where the painter's skilful use of light, which enfolds and caresses the sleeping child, the face of the mother, and the flanks of the animal, projects a sense of emotional involvement. This highly realistic glimpse of rural life, poetic in its simplicity, reaffirms the universal and symbolic value of motherhood.

Vincenzo Gemito,
Il pescatore
(The Fisherman)

This lovely bronze statue is one of the many very young fishermen portrayed in the later 19th century by the expressive Neapolitan artist.

Galleria d'Arte Moderna

In 1921, the Galleria d'Arte Moderna (Gallery of Modern Art) founded in 1868 and enlarged over the years thanks to bequests and donations, was installed in the elegant, resplendent rooms of the majestic Villa Reale. The gallery, perforce rearranged in 1949 after the building had been damaged by the dramatic events of WW2, is today the repository of a great number of masterpieces and is ennobled by precious collections of Italian paintings—of the Lombard schools in particular—from the 1800's and the early 20th century. The star of the collection is, without a doubt, Giuseppe Pellizza da Volpedo's ultra-famous *The Fourth State* (1901). Arranged in scores of rooms on the ground and first floors of the villa, the collection also offers an interesting panorama of Neoclassical and Romantic sculpture, again Italian and again specifically of the Lombard schools. The prominent artists so worthily represented here are innumerable: from Francesco Hayez to Andrea Appiani, from Antonio Canova to Tranquillo Cremona, and from Giacomo Favretto to Giovanni Segantini and Medardo Rosso, to name just a few.

Amedeo Modigliani, *Portrait of the Art Dealer Paul Guillaume*

Painted in 1916, this portrait depicts Paul Guillaume, art critic, art dealer, and collector of contemporary and African art—but above all, the patron of the Livornese artist. And more yet, since he defined himself "Modigliani's only dealer in 1914, for all of 1915, and for a part of 1916." Paul Guillaume opened an art gallery in Rue de Miromesnil in 1914, but had begun to express an interest in the work of Modigliani the year before, when the poet Max Jacob had introduced the two men. Essentially, Modigliani was a portrait painter— and he painted almost all the important figures he encountered during his short but eventful and impassioned existence, which he spent between Montmartre and Montparnassse. The Tuscan artist's portrayal of Paul Guillaume exasperates the elements typical of his patron's character: Guillaume was a cultured, refined man, a snob as were all the art dealers of the era, with a dandy's expressions and poses. But in this painting there is no irony, and even less so, caricature: these expressions were not part of the universe of "Modi," the only "damned" artist of the twentieth century. Here we see only his need to interpret, to establish a sort of complicity with his patron. Most striking, in this geometrical portrait, is that "lost look," those blind eyes that do not focus on anything, here one different from the other: the left light-colored, watery; the other "sewn up" as though by a dark patch. A year later, he painted French painter of Russian origin Léopold Survage in the same manner, and when Survage asked why, Modigliani is said to have answered, "Because with one eye you are looking at the world and with the other you are looking inside yourself."

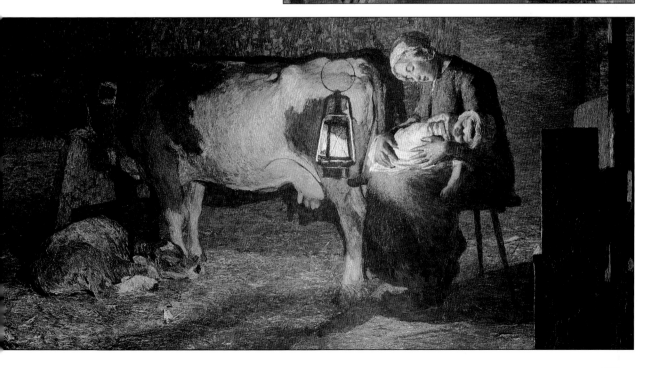

Corso Venezia

Once known as Corso di Porta Orientale, what is now Corso Venezia was, in the 1700's, the most fashionable street in Milan, the true heart of the city's lively society life. And today, echoes of it old role still linger in the well-defined architectural elegance of many of the facades of the aristocratic palazzi that line the street and those immediately adjacent to it. For example, the former *Seminario Vescovile* built by order of Saint Charles Borromeo in 1564, with its Baroque portal. Or the Renaissance *Casa Silvestri*, formerly *Fontana*, built in the late 1400's over earlier buildings (13th-14th century) and rising elegantly around a porticoed courtyard: it clearly evinces the influence of Bramante (if not his art itself); it was radically restored in 1961. But there is also the medieval *church of San Pietro Celestino*, with a single nave, restructured in Borromini's style and taste in 1735. And again, the 17th-century *Palazzo del Senato*, commissioned by Federico Borromeo and built by Francesco Maria Richini, and the coeval *Palazzo Serbelloni*, enlarged and renovated in Neoclassical style in 1793 by Simone Cantoni. History is a household word in Palazzo Serbelloni, in particular: in 1796 its halls hosted Napoleon, in 1838 Metternich, and in 1859 witnessed the meeting of two great historical figures, Vittorio Emanuele II and Napoleon III. Corso Venezia also figures importantly in literature: here, almost at the end of the broad, busy thoroughfare, stood that "Convento dei Cappuccini di Porta Orientale" made famous in the pages of Alessandro Manzoni's *The Betrothed*.

Corso Venezia, once known as Corso di Porta Orientale, is one of the city's longest and broadest avenues, lined by aristocratic mansions of great magnificence.

San Babila

Tradition has it that San Babila—Milan's oldest Christian church, having been built in 46 AD—stands on the site of an ancient pagan temple consecrated to the cult of the sun. It is said that the church was founded by Saint Barnabas, who also celebrated his first Mass in Milan here. Due to having been restructured many times in the course of its history, the architecture of San Babila unites Romanesque, Renaissance, and Baroque elements. The church was rebuilt and enlarged in 1575, acquired an impressive facade (later destroyed) in 1698-1610, the same period in which the Romanesque apses were completed; it was fully restored in 1880 in its 11th-century Romanesque style; the suggestive *facade* we see today was added by Cesare Nava in 1905. One of the important historical events linked to San Babila is the baptism of Alessandro Manzoni. In front of the entrance, in Piazza San Babila, stands the *Colonna del Leone* by Giuseppe Robecco (1626), topped by a stone lion: in times past it was probably the symbol of the Porta Orientale quarter.

The interior and exterior of the church of San Babila. Facing the church is the Colonna del Leone, created in 1626 by Giuseppe Robecco. This probable emblem of the ancient quarter of Porta Orientale is topped by a stone lion.

The Navigli, with their banks, their boats, their terraces, and of course their festivals are strongly representative of the romantic and in a certain sense historical aspects, as well as the popular traditions, of one of Europe's most modern and active cities.

Navigli

Since ancient times, Milan's system of *navigli* (canals) was a well-articulated network for handling complex transportation and communications problems. For example, a large part of the most unwieldy and hard-to-transport materials for the construction of the Duomo (not least, marble slabs and stone) moved along these waterways, efficiently managed by a system of sluices and basins (of note, those of Sant'Eustorgio, more or less in correspondence to today's Darsena di Porta Ticinese, and of Santo Stefano) that which made it possible—when required—to regulate the water level to facilitate navigation by the heavy barges. Very little survives today of the ancient system that linked Milan to the outlying areas. One such leftover is the *Darsena di Porta Ticinese*, the only remaining basin and once one of Italy's major river ports, 750 meters in length; its construction began in 1603. The Darsena is still connected to the Naviglio Grande, running from Abbiategrasso, and the Naviglio Pavese, which joins the river Ticino after having flowed through Pavia. The latter waterway was designed in the early 1300's, but the history of Milan's navigli is older than that: it goes back almost a thousand years, since apparently the first navigable stretch of canal dates to the second half of the 12th century. At the beginning, it was a question of trade: the land around the city had to be irrigated, a valid alternative to the existing road system (at the time unsafe and difficult to travel) was sorely needed, and it was imperative to provide a fast, direct link between the Alpine passes and the lakes with Milan—and eventually with the sea. The first canal to be inaugurated (1179), the Ticinello, about 50 kilometers in length, was the laboriously-built prelude to construction of the *Naviglio Grande*. This was an ambitious project, and one that was extremely demanding for the technology of the era—and in fact, as the work proceeded, many illustrious engineers were called in to contribute to the work. And not at all surprisingly, the innovative system of sluices that distinguish the navigli was designed in the late

More bridges, sluices, and craft on the quiet canals that create the extraordinary atmosphere of the evocative world of Milan's Navigli.

Ancient wash-houses built on the secondary canals of the Navigli are testimony to the customs of the harder life of times past. Lovingly preserved, these structures lend a pleasingly rétro cast to these charming corners of old Milan.

1400's by no less than Leonardo da Vinci. The canals naturally had the effect of changing the face of the city as they penetrated further and further into the urban fabric; but Milan's economy also changed and expanded, thanks above all to easier communications and therefore trade opportunities. Hay, wood, forage, coal, livestock, cheeses, and much more came to the city by the water route; wine, salt, grain, and various manufactured goods departed toward Switzerland. In 1805, Napoleon completed construction of the *Naviglio Pavese*—ordered by Gian Galeazzo Visconti and only partially built by the time of Galeazzo Maria Sforza—and so assured Milan a direct link with the sea via the river Po. Another canal, the *Naviglio della Martesana* united the city with Lake Como via the river Adda designed by Filippo Maria Visconti as an irrigation canal also suitable for navigation, it was built by Francesco Sforza in 1457-1465. These three great navigli are the only ones to have survived the far-reaching, complex work of filling the canals that began in the late 19th century and continued into the early years of the next. Almost everything disappeared: besides the canals themselves, the quays, the bridges, the barges, and much of the typical architecture that lent a special identity not only to the urban fabric but also to the surrounding territory, distinguished by its orderly stands of poplars, ricefields, isolated farmhouses, abbeys, and small villages. As we have said, the only survivors were the Naviglio Grande, the Naviglio Pavese, and a few hundred meters of the Naviglio della Martesana. All that remains today of the great Darsena is the loop along the Spanish walls, where the barges once tied up to be loaded and unloaded. But something else still lives on, in grand style: the atmosphere and the spirit of the navigli, the characteristic quarter of the old Milan that reflects in the waters where barges still float; there are innumerable cafés, trattorias, restaurants, and crafts and antique shops that attract the Milanese, tourists, and simple curiosity-seekers with their special and timeless charm. And there has also survived the tradition of the local markets: the *Fiera di Sinigallia*, held on Saturdays, with its rows of stalls and booths along the Darsena, and the antiques market, which every last Sunday of the month draws crowds to the Naviglio Grande. In early June every year, the popular *Festa dei Navigli* inevitably infects the whole city with its festive air as its celebrates this unique corner of Milan.

The church of San Cristoforo sul Naviglio and more views of city's ancient watercourses.

Top, typical homes directly on the Naviglio Grande; right, the picturesque Vicolo dei Lavandai; bottom, a beautiful view of the Naviglio della Martesana.

Sant'Eustorgio

Eustorgius, a personality so famous as to have become the subject of legend, lived in the 4th century and was the ninth Bishop of Milan. His foremost merit lay in having made an adventurous journey to Constantinople and to have carried back to Milan the sacred relics of the Three Kings, donated by the emperor of the East. And even though Frederick Barbarossa carried the relics off to Cologne (from whence only a small portion returned to Milan in 1903), the tradition of their veneration was by that time so deeply rooted in Milan's populace that each year, on Epiphany, a procession set out (and still does) from the Duomo to pay homage in the ancient basilica named for the sainted bishop. And it is still from Sant'Eustorgio that each new bishop, on the day of his installation in office, begins his transfer to the Duomo of Milan. In Sant'Eustorgio, Ludovico il Moro and his court welcomed Ludovico's betrothed, Beatrice d'Este, with a grand wedding procession. The great church, built in the 6th century by order of Bishop Eustorgius II on the site of an older building believed to have been raised by his predecessor of the same name, was rebuilt in Romanesque style in the 11th century but was razed to the ground in 1164 by Frederick Barbarossa, who carried off what tradition considered to be the bodies of the three Magi. The church was later entirely rebuilt and while portions dating to the 13th century still stand (for example, the *bell tower*, with its typical Lombard forms), most of the architecture dates to the 14th and 15th centuries. Even the chapels, which run along the right side as far as the apse, are in clear chronological succession. Of particular note is the splendid **Portinari Chapel** (1462-1468), with precious decorations by

Top, an overall view of the Portinari Chapel.

Foppa; it was innovative for the times and a ground-breaking example of refined Renaissance architecture—but also proof of the level of magnificence attained by that time by the wealthy middle-class clients and sponsors. The chapel was built for the Florentine Pigello Portinari, and some experts would even have it the Michelozzo was involved in its construction. It was more proba-

The plain gabled facade of the church of Sant'Eustorgio; center, a detail of the architrave of the main portal.

bly designed by a Lombard artist, who gave it a square body, marked at the corners by aediculae and with a polygonal tambour and a cupola. At the center of the chapel stands the resplendent *Ark of Saint Peter Martyr* by Giovanni di Balduccio, who trained in the workshop of Giovanni Pisano; it was created in 1336-1339 on order from Azzone Visconti. In fact, the basilica, part of a larger complex embracing the ancient Dominican monastery—built on the site of a ancient hospital, seat from 1228 of the Court of the Inquisition and for a long time under the protection of the Visconti family—has ties with the cult of Saint Peter Martyr (Peter of Verona), a Dominican friar, a fiery preacher, and an inflexible Inquisitor, who lived in the monastery in the mid-13th century. In that same century, the presence of the Dominicans dictated extensive restructuring work and redecoration of the church and assured the highly prestigious role that the sacred building was to play in the religious life of the city in the centuries that followed.

The *facade* of the basilica, remodeled in 1862-1865 in pseudo-Romanesque gabled style according to typical Lombard criteria, is quite austere, in harmony with the interior, with a nave and two aisles and a broad apse, spacious and cleanly linear but embellished with extraordinary masterpieces of paint-ing and sculpture. Think, for example, of the *Gothi tomb of Stefano Visconti*, another work by Giovann di Balduccio, or the unfinished Gothic *altar fronta* in marble, with the *Stories of the Passion of Chris* that rises behind the main altar, or the frescoes tha decorate the chapels, the sarcophagi, the statue: and, naturally, the *Chapel of the Magi*—all of whic make this church a true treasure-chest of ines timable value.

The heavy aerial bombing of 15 August 1943 ha serious repercussions on the complex and above a on the cloisters of the ancient monastery; the firs less damaged portion was restored almost immedi ately; the second, much more seriously hit, only i the period 1987-2001. In the second case the work were conducted with in mind the plan, toda brought to fruition, to use the cloister as a *Diocesa Museum*, which now proposes some of the most pre cious ecclesiastical treasures in all Lombardy. I 2000, substantial restoration work was also con ducted on the Dominicans' ancient *Sala Capitola* (Chapter Hall) and on the facade of the basilica.

Almost as if to remind us of the central role playe by this basilica, the square in front is still graced b the legendary font at which Saint Barnabas is sai to have begun baptizing in Milan, thus official marking the birth of the local Church.

Below, a detail of the exuberant Ark of Saint Peter Martyr in t Portinari Chapel, also the home of the beautiful fresco l Vincenzo Foppa, shown on the facing page, of Saint Peter Mart overthrowing the Devil with the Ho

San Lorenzo Maggiore alle Colonne

In the Porta Ticinese quarter, behind 16 marbl
Corinthian columns (the remains of a Roman build
ing—palace, temple, or baths—brought to Milan i
the 4th century to make up a part of the four-side
portico that originally stood before the church), ris
es the basilica of San Lorenzo Maggiore all
Colonne, a building that offers precious evidence c
what early-Christian Milan was like. The broa
church courtyard with the *bronze statue of Empero
Constantine*, a copy of an Roman original in th
Lateran, opens out behind the columns and be
tween the two presbyteries. More than once de
stroyed, rebuilt, and restored, today's church in
cludes Romanesque (12th-century) and Renais

ance additions, a 16th-17th century cupola, and a 19th-century facade. But the original structure, from the 4th-5th century, on a central plan (partially transformed into an octagon by Martino Bassi, who restructured the church in 1573 following a disastrous collapse) with the apses inscribed in a square (a fact which leads us to believe the plan was Byzantine in inspiration) and four corner towers, is still clearly visible and just as clearly early-Christian in matrix. Also early-Christian are the three *chapels* (4th-6th century), still decorated with coeval *mosaics* and *frescoes*: the *Chapel of Saint Aquilinus*, on an octagonal plan with niches and women's galleries, and the chapels of *Saint Hippolytus* and *Saint Sixtus*.

The images on these two pages are highly representative of the variety of styles that distinguishes the vast complex of San Lorenzo Maggiore. On the facing page: top, the columns in front of the church, from which it takes its alternative name of San Lorenzo alle Colonne; left and bottom, two panoramic views that place in sharp relief the play of volumes that typify this complex.
On this page, clockwise; the statue of Constantine, the interior of a cupola, a view of the church, the Rape of Elijah, a 4th-5th century mosaic in the Chapel of Sant'Aquilino, where we also find the frescoes and the Roman sarcophagus shown in the last two images.

Santa Maria presso San Satiro

An authentic masterpiece by Donato Bramante, the basilica of Santa Maria presso San Satiro, unassumingly set in a recess among the colorful shops of Via Torino, rises on the site of a 9th-century church that was more than once renovated but totally restructured and enlarged only beginning in 1478. The work, sponsored by Gian Galeazzo Sforza, was dictated by the need to ensure a more suitable and safer home for a venerated image of the Virgin that had previously stood in a small chapel where it had been brutally disfigured in September of 1477. This was the first Milanese worksite for a Bramante at the time not more than thirty, who had been attracted to Milan by the construction of the Duomo and who in San Satiro worked for more than 10 years. The result was an elegant building that preserved, connected to the left transept, the *sacellum* erected in 876 by then-archbishop Anspert in honor of saints Ambrose, Sylvester, and Satyrus. It was transformed, in the 15th century—perhaps by the hand of Leonardo—into the *Chapel of the Pietà*, on a plan still Byzantine in derivation, with an octagonal cupola crowned by a small lantern. However, the space for the new church was inevitably restricted by the presence, to the east, of the narrow Via del Falcone. And thus, since it was impossible to expand the structure (and in particular, to build the choir of the church) in that direction, the able decorator and expert painter Bramante succeeded in making there seem to be volume where none existed: in the interior, he created a masterful *trompe-l'œil* of a "virtual" presbytery and three great arches with lacunar vaults by simple painting. Historians and architects have long debated over the various phases in the construction of the elegant building and the evolution of the Latin cross plan with a nave and two aisles and a broad barrel-vaulted transept, which in the end created three volumes on square plans arranged symmetrically around the central body. But Bramante's greatest merit here surely lay in his ability to lend to the forms an air of spaciousness that the small size of the complex would never have permitted by normal architectural means. The church has two *facades*, one on Via del Falcone and the other, principal facade, set back from the roadway on Via Torino; this facade was first designed by Giovanni Antonio Amadeo in 1486, but plans were revised over time and it was finally completed in Renaissance style, by Giuseppe Vandoni only in 1870. Above, a large hemispherical dome crowns the complex. On the right side (on Via Torino) it is flanked by an interesting *sacristy*, topped by another, flat, cupola; the building, again Bramante's work, is adorned with a fine *frieze* in polychrome terracotta by Agostino De Fondutis and in its octagonal form recalls the baptisteries of Romanesque matrix. The *bell tower*, ornamented by a play of small cantilever arches and two-light windows, dates to the 11th century and may be considered the model for the Lombard Romanesque bell towers.

Two views of the interior of the church of Santa Maria presso San Satiro: above, the baptismal font and, left, the main altar.

Santa Maria presso San Celso

Preceded by an austere four-sided portico and also known as Santa Maria dei Miracoli, this church was designed by Giangiacomo Dolcebuono in 1493 as a single-nave building on a Latin-cross plan, surmounted by a cupola, but it was actually built, over the course of almost a century, in a felicitous Renaissance style incorporating a series of substantial modifications and much enlarged with respect to the original plan. Just think that contributing to the work (and to its successful conclusion) were, one after the other, Cristoforo Solari and Giovanni Antonio Amadeo, Cesare Cesariano (to whom we owe the elegant atrium), Lombardino (Cristoforo Lombardo), Bernardino Zenale and Vincenzo Seregni, and Galeazzo Alessi and Martino Bassi. As to the name, the church owes it to the small *church of San Celso*, built in the 10th century on the site of the saint's martyrdom and today practically snuggled against the more majestic newer sacred building. The facade is a dense forest of columns, pilaster strips, windows, caryatids, statue, reliefs, and niches, into which three portals penetrate. The interior was finally built with a nave and two aisles under gilded coffered ceilings, stuccowork, and frescoes. At the *Altar of the Virgin* to the left of the presbytery, with on it a *statue of Our Lady of the Assumption* by Annibale Fontana (1586), brides traditionally come to pray on their wedding day. Behind we still find the remains of the *fresco of a miraculous Virgin* around which the church was originally built. The notable wooden *choir*, with magnificent decorations and inlays, was created in 1570 by Paolo Gaza to drawings by Galeazzo Alessi.

Santa Maria presso San Celso. On the left, the Santuario di Santa Maria dei Miracoli and, right, the Romanesque church of San Celso.

San Carlo al Corso

Clean-cut and resplendent in its linear Classicism, the basilica of San Carlo al Corso stands triumphant at the back of an elegant small square. It was built by Carlo Amati in 1832-1837 on a central plan, and is surmounted by a sober dome (1844) designed by Felice Pizzagalli, who rested it on a high drum enlivened by half-columns, windows, and niches. The basilica is introduced by a graceful pronaos topped by an essential pediment, in the most perfect Neoclassical style. Vaguely inspired by the Roman Pantheon, the interior is a chorus of columns, pillars, niches, and chapels, and is exemplary for the sumptuous richness of its decoration (for example, the 15th-century Lombard *Nativity*, in relief, to the right of the main entrance; and *The Apotheosis of Saint Charles* in the vault of the presbytery) as well as for the important works of art it houses (for example, a group by Pompeo Marchesi representing *Saint Luigi Gonzaga receiving Communion from Saint Charles* and the *statue of the Virgin* moved here from the pre-existing church of Santa Maria dei Servi, linked to the adjoining monastery of the Servite fathers).

The Classical-style church of San Carlo al Corso, built by Carlo Amati, in Corso Vittorio Emanuele.

DEDICATVM S. CAROLO MDCCCXLVII

A view of the cloister known in the past as the Lazzaretto.

The Lazzaretto

The ancient site of the Lazzaretto (lazar house) is still easy to identify due to the presence, at its center, of the **church of San Carlo al Lazzaretto**, built by order of Saint Charles Borromeo in 1585, on an octagonal plan with openings on all eight sides to permit the faithful to observe the priest officiating the Mass from wherever they happened to be. The Lazzaretto itself was originally a four-sided building of considerable size (378 x 370 m), which embraced and delimited a vast inner area where for centuries those afflicted with the plague were assembled and, if possible, treated. It was built by order of Ludovico il Moro, who in 1488 awarded the commission to Lazzaro Palazzi; it was completed in 1506 but restructured in 1629. The immense complex and the ill fame that surrounded it were made famous by Manzoni's description of the terrible plague of 1630 in the pages of his *The Betrothed*. The name of the complex is, however, also linked to other equally important but certainly less tragic events, like the proclamation of the Cisalpine Republic within its walls on 9 July 1797 in the presence of Napoleon and the then-archbishop of Milan, Filippo Visconti. Destroyed in the late 1800's, the Lazzaretto was replaced by housing, which has by now occupied the entire area.

San Nazaro Maggiore

This austere basilica was founded in about 386 by Saint Ambrose on the site of a Christian cemetery; the bishop dedicated it to the Apostles, some of whose relics were kept here. When to these were added the relics of Saint Nazarius, the entire church was rededicated with the name by which we know it yet today. It was razed more than once by violent fires (including the truly disastrous fire of 1075) and rebuilt, with a tambour and dome. Remodeled in the 16th century, unfortunately restored in the 1800's by Pietro Pestagalli, who jeopardized precious original structures to replace them with Neoclassical elements, and laboriously but accurately restored in the period 1938-1962 (despite the tragic parenthesis of the war), the church has won back its original simplicity. The early-Christian perimeter has been recovered, as have been dedicatory tablets, the ancient inscriptions, and even the tomb of Saint Nazarius. Further restoration work (1967-1986) returned a number of Romanesque elements, the sacristies, and the crypt by Bramantino to their original splendor. Bramantino was also the author (in his only documented architectural work) of the large *Trivulzio Funeral Chapel*, commissioned in 1512 by Gian Giacomo Trivulzio and today the monumental vestibule that gives access to the basilica.

The church of San Nazaro Maggiore. Top, the ... of the Tr... al Chapel; center, the to... of the church

(cropped)

San Simpliciano

This ancient basilica, ordered by Saint Ambrose in the 4th century, was completed only by his successor, that Saint Simplicianus who was buried here alongside the relics of three venerated martyrs, Alexander, Martyrius, and Sissinius. Since that time, much has changed in the basilica, with especially significative actions between the 7th and the 11th century. Behind the gabled facade, restored in 1870, is a Romanesque church (the apse, the tambour, and the bell tower date to the 12th century). The church is still remembered in connection with the Battle of Legnano, won, according to tradition, due to the intervention of the three saints martyr who are buried here and recalled in the *stained-glass windows*.

Three details of the facade of the church of San Simpliciano.

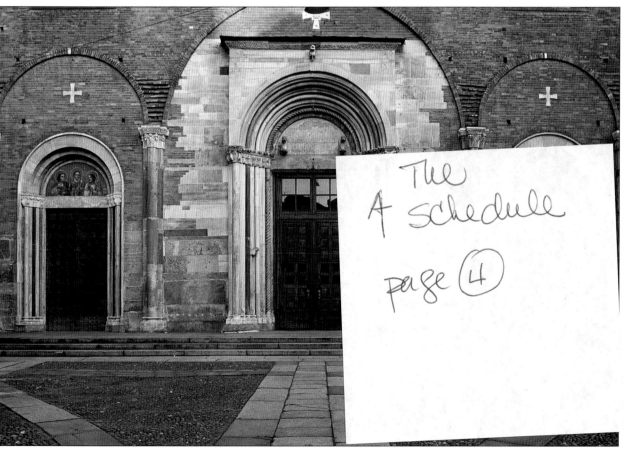

MODERN-DAY MILAN

All around the world, thinking of present-day Milan, the image that most always comes to people's minds is of a modern city at the avant-garde, so industrious as to be almost untiring, in the sway of frenetic rhythms, innovative ideas, and, naturally, armies of managers and businessmen. It is the Milan of soaring buildings and busy streets, of modern infrastructures and new technologies: the Milan of 2000. And even this Milan has its "historical" symbols.

Fiera di Milano

If Milan is considered to be the economic capital of Italy, the Fiera cannot be anything but its pulsing heart. It all started in 1920, when the first "Fiera Campionaria" was held on the Porta Venezia ramparts; only three years later, the Fiera was transferred to its presence quarters in Via Domodossola. The site grew over time to embrace the 26 *pavilions* that stand there today, on an area of more than 375,000 square meters. Today, the once-great and historical "Fiera Campionaria" has been replaced with a well-articulated series of smaller trade fairs and annual events, all more or less sector-specialized, which have made this exhibition center one of the major points of reference in Europe for business.

The skyscraper housing the State Railway headquarters.

Bottom, the new entrance to the "Fiera Campionaria".

Stazione Centrale

Begun in 1906 to plans by the architect Ulisse Stacchini as part of a wider-reaching project to reorganize and rationalize rail transport, but completed and inaugurated only in 1931, Milan's Stazione Centrale or Central Station is extraordinarily rich in ornamentation and decorative elements, from the reliefs to the sculptural groups and to the medallions that adorn its walls. The front of the station, 207 meters in breadth, is entirely clad in stone and flanked by two wings stretch parallel to the tracks. The enormous metal canopies, visible only in part from the gallery inside the station, are particularly spectacular elements of the station architecture.

One of the winged horses that adorn the Stazione Centrale, of which the facade on Via Vittor Pisani is visible at the bottom.

Stadio Giuseppe Meazza

When, in the 1920's, the industry baron Piero Pirelli entertained the idea of creating a sports facilities center in Milan, he commissioned the architects Ulisse Stacchini and Alberto Cugini to draw up plans for a huge stadium to be used only for soccer (and therefore, with no track), with four linear *grandstands* (two along the short sides and two along the long sides of the field) not connected by curves and set very close to the playing field. The Stadio di San Siro was thus inaugurated on 19 September 1926; it had cost 5 million lire of the time and had a 35,000 spectator capacity (with a 25,000 seating capacity); it was originally planned that the stadium host only the Milan team's home games, but it later also became the home of their "cousins" of Inter, the city's other soccer team. The stadium was purchased in 1935 by the city and soon acquired four *curves* connecting up the stands. Ten years or so later, however, the city decided to implement an ambitious plan by Calzolari and Ronca to further upgrade the structure by adding a *second tier*, which upped the spectator capacity to 100,000, with 70,000 seated. The new San Siro stadium, inaugurated in 1956, boasted perfect illumination for night games and partial roofing. When the World Soccer Championships were held in Italy in 1990, the structure, which by that time had borne the name

Three views of the Stadio Giuseppe Meazza, formerly San Siro. It is now practically enclosed in the structure supporting the futuristic third tier.

Giuseppe Meazza for ten years, was again upgraded with the addition of a *third tier* to plans by the architects Ragazzi and Hoffner: the new stands do not rest on the pre-existing ones but are rather supported by independent support structures that effectively surround the old stadium in its entirety. Four 51-meter high *corner towers* underpin a roof that protects all of the 85,700 seats from the rain. An interesting *museum* inside the stadium illustrates the history, the victories, and the exploits of Milan's two soccer teams.

Piazzale Cadorna

Piazzale Cadorna, an important node in the city road network in the Castello Sforzesco area, since 1999 has also been the site of the terminal of the railway line that links the city to the Malpensa international airport. For the occasion, Gae Aulenti was called in to adapt the old *Stazione delle Ferrovie Nord* (which had already been restructured in 1956) to its new use. In the square, the colorful monument entitled *Needle, Thread, and Knot*, by Claes Oldenburg stands as an emblem of the complex work of "darning" the transport system, and therefore also of evolution of the life of the city in general.

Claes Oldenburg's modern, brightly-colored sculpture entitled Needle, Thread, and Knot *stands in Piazzale Cadorna*

Torre Velasca

In many ways recalling the massive fortified structures of medieval times, and at the same time a daring project of exquisitely modern architecture, the
Torre Velasca soars to 106 meters, like a might
medieval tower house or a fortress magically transformed into a skyscraper, above the Milan skyline
Built between 1957 and 1960 to plans (and after
prolonged study) by the architects Banfi, Belgiojoso
Peressutti, and Rogers, the tower, with its characteristic mushroom shape, is a highly successful example of Rationalism in the urban environment. And
what to say of the designers' volition to distance
their creation from the model of the typical Amer-
can skyscraper in glass and iron, to embrace elements that are typical of Milanese architecture
from the proportions of the projecting elements t
the sizes of the windows, from the color shadings t
distribution of functions that so liken the tower t
the ancient medieval palaces: the lower floors are
in fact, occupied by offices and shops (as in time
past they were by storehouses and workshops); th
higher floors (since time immemorial typically res-
dential) by apartments.

Piazza Meda

Set in the very heart of Milan, this square acts i
the urban context as a bridge between the ancier
and the modern, between the traditional and the innovative. At its center, the huge bronze sculptur
by Arnaldo Pomodoro entitled *Il Sole* ("The Sun"
and, at the corner with Via Case Rotte, the *Chas
Manhattan Bank* building, designed by the architectural studio of Banfi, Belgiojoso, Peressutti, an
Rogers, with its unmistakable and quite spectacula
curved facade.

Grattacielo Pirelli

Built in 1955-1959 on the site where the first Pirel
factory had stood since 1872, this skyscrape
Italy's tallest and one of the
tallest in Europe, was designed by Giò Ponti with
the collaboration of the
architects Fornaroli, Ros-
selli, Valtolina, Dell'Orto, and the great Pier
Luigi Nervi. By now, it
has become an authen-
tic symbol of Milan. The
building, in reinforced
concrete, rises to 127 meters; it is renowned for the
elegance and uncluttered lin-
earity of its modern architectural forms.

*Top, the Torre Velasca, soaring to 106 meters just a few
hundred meters from the Duomo.
Another of the many modern elements in the Lombard
capital is a sculpture by Arnaldo Pomodoro entitled* Il
Sole, *in Piazza Meda (left and above).*

Left, the Grattacielo Pirelli, affectionately called "il Pirellone."
Top right and bottom, other beautiful examples of contemporary
architecture: the first in the Giambellino quarter, the second
near San Siro.

The Architecture of Today and Tomorrow

During the course of its unstoppable urban development, Milan has seen the nascence of whole new neighborhoods, structural revisitation of existing quarters on the outskirts, reorganization of industrial areas, residential areas, and green areas, and the birth of a truly great technological center in the Pirelli-Bicocca area (the well-known *Tecnocity*). Modern architecture, the functionality of the whole, and rational organization were the strands in the guiding thread of this extraordinary process of growth and innovation. The end result?

Buildings expressing definite personalities while still adhering to the criteria of extreme and rational Modernism, a truly new city, a celebration in counterpoint to the historical, traditional center; and here and there, clear and quite fascinating points of contact between the past and the future. Think, for example, of the splendid *Cavallo di Leonardo* at the entrance to the *Ippodromo di San Siro* (the racetrack complex created in 1915). The statue was based on drawings by the extraordinary genius from Vinci, who during the time he spent in Milan designed, in a long and impassioned creative process—but without ever attaining any "concrete" results—an enormous horse. The idea of bringing Leonardo's creature "to life" was enthusiastically supported by Charles Dent, a former US pilot who even established a foundation for the prime purpose of ensuring its realization; unfortunately, he died in 1994, five years before the work was completed. The horse was donated to the City of Milan, which installed it where we all can still admire it today. And again, the *Stazione di Porta Garibaldi*, built in 1960-1963 to replace the old Stazione di Porta Nuova and today dominated by the elegant profile of the *Torre dell'Acquedotto*.

Milan's strong vocation for everything modern does not exclude attention to the historical. Below, the modern-day realization of the horse designed by Leonardo da Vinci, installed at the San Siro racetrack complex. Top left, buildings in Tecnocity; top right, low-rent housing in the Gratosoglio quarter. Bottom right, the Torre dell'Acquedotto at the Porta Garibaldi railroad station.

The austere and simply-designed church of the Abbazia di Chiaravalle, with its large portico before the facade and the mighty lateral buttresses, stands in the charming setting of the green countryside near Milan.

Abbazia di Chiaravalle

A short distance outside Milan, 5 kilometers south-east of the city, rises one of the first and most important Cistercian monasteries, founded, on 22 January 1135 with the support of the population of Milan, by Saint Bernard of Clairvaux (Chiaravalle in Italian), from whom the abbey took its name. At the time, the area was desolate and swampy, but in a short time the tenacious work of the friars succeeded in reclaiming it and making area one of the most important artistic and religious centers in the Italy of the time. Since 1465 held in commendam by Cardinal Ascanio Sforza, son of Duke Francesco, with time the influence and the wealth of the abbey declined, especially under Spanish administration. In 1768 the friars were forced to abandon the monastery, which in the following decades suffered damage (if not outright ruin). The friars returned only in 1953, when they immediately and with great conviction began an attempt to reconstruct the ancient structure. But by that time, all that remained of the earlier monumental complex was the church, consecrated in 1221, with its mighty buttresses along the sides, the stately transept and the

lantern supporting the original 14th-century *tower* (the other bell tower dates instead to 1568). The sacred building is notable for the way its architecture blends motifs of clearly French matrix with Romanesque elements and elements from the Lombard tradition; the interior, with a nave and two aisles separated by pillars and crowned by the ogival arches typical of the Cistercian Gothic, is resplendent with decorations by masters of the one of the Tuscan schools, perhaps Sienese, perhaps even Giotto's. To them we owe, for example, the splendid cycle of frescoes illustrating the *Life of the Virgin*, dating probably to the early 14th century. Other pictorial works are traceable to the hands of the Fiammenghini, a family of artists active in the 16th and 17th centuries. To the same era are attributable various works involving remodeling of the façade, with its large portico in front, and the square on which few buildings still standing on it. Other "survivors" are the ancient *cemetery* adjacent to the church and a portion of the 13th-century *cloister*, in Gothic style, on which face the restored 14th-century *refectory* and the radically restructured *Sala Capitolare* or Chapter Hall.

Left, the imposing bell tower seen from the interior of the cloister, of which a suggestive image is presented below. On the facing page, a view of the nave with the splendid wooden choir in the foreground, and three images of the beautiful cycle of frescoes that decorates the interior of the church.

Index